# Sorcerers of
# STONE

"In *Sorcerers of Stone*, Camille Sauvé conjures up a visionary and transformative archaeological experience. She guides her readers deeply into the magical world of mysterious megalithic monuments with a focus on Peru and Bolivia. Going beyond the imposing physicality of these perplexing lapidary manifestations, she takes us into more esoteric topics such as sonic manipulation of stone, advanced human life in distant ages, and more."

MICHAEL A. CREMO, AUTHOR OF *FORBIDDEN ARCHEOLOGY*

"Camille Sauvé delivers an important contribution toward unraveling the mysteries of the spectacular monoliths and megaliths of the ancient sacred sites of Peru. The sheer size and technical sophistication of these sites has puzzled explorers and archaeologists for centuries. Who built these structures, when were they built, and what was their original purpose? Camille explores a number of diverse subjects that are not often combined by scholars, such as oral history, culture, masonry, shamanic practices, and metaphysics, in an attempt to get a better comprehension regarding the true origins of these breathtaking sites. *Sorcerers of Stone* is a major contribution to this sector of literature and research."

MICHAEL TELLINGER, AUTHOR OF
*AFRICAN TEMPLES OF THE ANUNNAKI*

# Sorcerers of STONE

## ARCHITECTS OF THE THREE AGES

### CAMILLE M. SAUVÉ

Bear & Company
Rochester, Vermont

Bear & Company
One Park Street
Rochester, Vermont 05767
www.BearandCompanyBooks.com

Text stock is SFI certified

Bear & Company is a division of Inner Traditions International

Cataloging-in-Publication Data for this title is available from the Library of Congress

ISBN 978-1-59143-508-2 (print)
ISBN 978-1-59143-509-9 (ebook)

Printed and bound in the United States by Lakebook Manufacturing, LLC
The text stock is SFI certified. The Sustainable Forestry Initiative® program promotes sustainable forest management.

10  9  8  7  6  5  4  3  2  1

Text design and layout by Virginia Scott Bowman
This book was typeset in Garamond Premier Pro with Geographica Hand used as the display typeface
Photographs by Camille M. Sauvé unless otherwise noted

To send correspondence to the author of this book, mail a first-class letter to the author c/o Inner Traditions • Bear & Company, One Park Street, Rochester, VT 05767, and we will forward the communication, or contact the author through her website **sorcerersofstone.com**.

Scan the QR code and save 25% at InnerTraditions.com. Browse over 2,000 titles on spirituality, the occult, ancient mysteries, new science, holistic health, and natural medicine.

♦♦♦

*In gratitude to all the ancient builders who
left their incredible marks on our landscape.
I hope we learn from the invaluable secrets
that lie within these sites.*

# Contents

## PART 3

# Rending the Veil:
# Visions from the Akashic

## PART 4

# Reexamining Our History

✦✦✦

# Acknowledgments

I am eternally grateful to Francisco P. Carbajal who has been my travel companion during the wonderful odyssey of creating of this book. He has helped enormously dealing with some of the difficulties in logistics, and communication, here in Peru. Many of his beautiful photographs grace the pages within this book.

A very special thanks to my friend Jenny P. Miller who helped me with the initial proofing and editing of this book. Her fabulous advice on which publishers would be most interested in my book was spot on, and her recommendation of the highly knowledgeable and helpful agent Andy Ross was a godsend. I would highly recommend her to anyone needing editing work. You can contact her at: jenevamiller@yahoo.com.

I would also like to thank Scott Page, my good friend, who gave me great advice and encouragement. With the exacting eye of a seasoned architect, he gave important insights into archaeology and architecture that initially escaped my notice.

Thanks to my amazing son, Adam, for his help in explaining some of the more obtuse math and science concepts in this book, abilities he obviously got from his father.

With special acknowledgment to Jesus Gamarra and Jan Peter de Jong who have been very helpful in conveying many of the concepts of the late Alfredo Gamarra, and for providing many photos in this book.

Special kudos to Vladimir Kundin whose has made a wonderful body of YouTube videos about ancient sites around the world, many

I would have never heard about if I didn't serendipitously land on his channel, "Vlad9vt."

Thanks to all the people who allowed me to use their photography in this book, including Bruno Teste, whose wonderful photos fill the section about Fountaineblau, Guilia Marchetti, Dave Woetzel, Marco Vigato, and all the people who have given permission to use their photos through creative commons licensing.

I would like to thank the wonderful staff at Inner Traditions. It was their professionalism and expertise that got this book polished enough for the market. I learned through the grueling, yet necessary, editing process just how invaluable a good publisher is for serious writers.

And, finally, in gratitude to all the ancient builders who left their incredible marks on our landscape. I hope we learn from the invaluable secrets that lie within these sites.

# Introduction

*The most beautiful experience we can have is the
mysterious. It is the fundamental emotion that stands at
the cradle of true art and true science.*

ALBERT EINSTEIN

There are thousands of mysterious rock formations around the
world that archaeologists and historians have a hard time explaining, as they don't seem to fit into any known building styles of early
human culture. Their designs are so abstract and enigmatic, these formations seem to be from a different world, and the modern mind can
only speculate as to their true purpose.

Where I live, in the Cusco region in Peru, these shrines are commonly referred to as *wakas* (sometimes spelled *huacas*), and one frequently sees locals and the occasional tourist visiting and exploring
them. Sometimes you will encounter shamans and spiritually inclined
persons making offerings of coca leaves, flowers, and fruits within a
carved niche or cave within the waka itself. Though wakas can take
many forms—including those that are natural, like boulders, caves,
mountains, springs, and trees—the sites I am specifically referring to
here are those that are obviously sculpted.

The forms on these mainly limestone monolithic rocks are shaped
into the most bizarre and delightful organic and geometric shapes.

Many of the wakas have stairs that go nowhere, hidden alcoves, water basins, canals, and recessed thrones, as well as the stepped-*chakana* symbol that is endemic around the Andes Mountains.

Some show animal forms molded into the rocks. Snakes are very prevalent, as are pumas and birds, although any creature's imagery is less common than abstract decorative forms.

Fig. i.1. The Grand Chincana, Sacsayhuaman, Peru.
Photo by Francisco Carbajal.

Another unique property of the wakas is that they look like the rocks were pressed or molded with ease, without any evidence of tool marks. Some sites show what appear to be finger pressings, where hands manipulated the stone to form canals and other shapes. Others are smoothed down to such a degree as to be as glossy as polished marble,

Fig. i.2. The Temple of the Condor at Machu Picchu.
See also color plate 1.

while others show signs of vitrification—a process that can only be done using high heat—resulting in a mirror-like reflective surface.

In many of these wakas, you can see they were designed for water flow and storage, and many have zigzagged canals winding down the rock. Almost all are built on or near tributaries and rivers, which may add to the site an energetic vitalizing life force called *camay* in Quechua. I believe this, combined with the properties within the stone itself, may facilitate the enhancement of one's consciousness (a topic that will be explored later in this book). Furthermore, many wakas are connected to intricate cave systems, which allegedly connect to key sites throughout Peru.

We also have evidence that these sites were revered as sacred by the later cultures that discovered them, so much so that they built protective walls and buildings around, near, or on top of them, in their own respective styles.

Fig. i.3. Zone X, Sacsayhuaman, a place
with an extensive cave system.

The late Peruvian researcher Alfredo Gamarra observed this, creating a classification system to designate the various types of ruins and wakas around Peru. Using this system, we see that the older, more abstract monolithic style that he refers to as *Hanan Pacha* ("heaven above, the First World Period) is frequently surrounded by the iconic polygonal megalithic style called *Uran Pacha* ("land of heaven below," the Second World Period). And often we see the *Ukun Pacha* building style ("land of heaven inside," the more recent period of the Incas, Killke, and Wari, according to Gamarra) constructed around, and on top of, these two other styles. What we are viewing is unmistakable: a visual timeline of overbuilding that portrays the presence of different cultures layered over different time periods.

Unfortunately, not much is written about these Hanan Pacha sites that gives any clarity as to who the builders were, although the ubiquitous response by the Peruvian Ministry of Culture-trained guides, archaeologists, and historians is that the Incas built them,

Fig. i.4. Uran Pacha overbuilding on Hanan Pacha monolith,
Pisac, Peru.
See also color plate 2.

especially in the period when Pachacuti Inca Yupanqui was emperor (1438–71 CE).

This is rather implausible for four key reasons.

- First, these sites are unlike any known Incan buildings in style or function.
- Second, most of these wakas are metamorphosed limestone, which is extremely hard to shape, and since the tools the Inca had were either made from bronze and copper, or were pounding stones, it seems very unlikely they could have pulled off the precision work seen on these wakas.
- Third, the quantity of wakas found around the area is enormous: there is an estimated count of over 328 wakas just in the Cusco area alone, and countless others throughout Peru, Bolivia, and Chile. Just where did Pachacuti and his son Tupac, and grandson Huascar, find the time in their short-lived empire (just

ninety-four years) to create so many wakas, especially since they were in warfare much of the time, not to mention maintaining a large empire?

- Fourth, and even more intriguingly, is that very similar rock formations are found in different parts of the world, as we can see in figures i.5, i.6, and i.7.

Fig. i.5. The Bomarzo pyramid of Italy features water canals and strange stairways similar to First World Period sites found in Peru.
Courtesy of Giulia Marchetti.

We can find similar constructions in Bulgaria, Japan, Italy, Portugal, China, and virtually anywhere we look (see chapter 14 for more examples). If one saw the sites in figures i.5, i.6, and i.7 here in Peru, one would not bat an eyelash, as they look like typical Peruvian Hanan Pacha work. But these are in countries very far away from Peru. What's going on here? Are we seeing evidence of a much larger, worldwide civilization?

Fig. i.6. Ancient quarry or a First World Period site?
Banbaura, Japan. Photo by JCastle, CC BY-NC-SA.
See also color plate 8.

Fig. i.7. The massive monoliths with iconic knobs
of Yangshan, China. 猫猫的日记本, CC BY-SA 4.0.

On top of this evidence, we can also find commentary by historians who were contemporaries of the Incas stating that the locals claimed they hadn't made these monuments but, in fact, had discovered them. The famous half-Inca, half-Spanish chronicler of the Incan empire Garcilaso de la Vega said this about the inexplicable site of Tiwanaku, a site near Lake Titicaca, which was the ancestral home of the Incas:

> I looked in wonder at a great wall built of such mighty stones that we could not imagine which earthly power could have been used to accomplish such a feat. . . . The natives maintain that the buildings were there before the Incas. . . . They do not know who the builders were, but know with some degree of certainty from their ancestors that all these wonders were erected in a single night.[1]

Spanish chronicler Pedro Cieza de Leon, who visited Tiwanaku in 1549, relates a similar account:

> In the presence of Juan Varagas, I asked the natives whether these buildings had been erected during the age of the Incas: they laughed and answered, the buildings had been there for many years before the Incas began their rule. These structures, they assured me, and they knew this with certainty from their forefathers, had been built in a single night, constructed by beings whose provenance they did not know. . . . And may the fame of these things remain intact throughout the universe . . . There were none still living who knew this unearthly site as anything other than ruins.[2]

In more recent times, these older, foundational Hanan and Uran Pacha styles have become the focus of a few alternative historians and researchers who claim that they are proof of a technically advanced, ancient civilization. Many of these revisionist historians claim the sites are antediluvian (pre-flood), and possibly Atlantean, as the rocks show advanced weather-related wear patterning.

There are a few who postulate an even older time period for these sites, one that would take them back to a much more ancient past than the most recent antediluvian times of about 12,000 years ago. Alfredo Gamarra, who first promoted the Cosmogony of the Three Worlds theory, along with his son, Jesús Gamarra, and Jesús's colleague Jan Peter de Jong, point out that these three different building styles correspond to three vast timelines of history. What is so fascinating about their theory is that, if correct, these sites would go back not hundreds or thousands of years, but hundreds of thousands, if not millions, of years in the past. Indeed, Sr. Gamarra's hypothesis is that these wakas were built at a time when the Earth was smaller and was in a closer orbit around the sun.

Most mainstream archaeologists and historians would scoff at this theory; however, I believe that because there is a lack of hard evidence that the Inca, Wari, or Killke made these stone monuments, and because we can see very similar structures all around the world, we should be open to exploring other theories. If we can keep an open but discerning mind, we may find some intriguing answers to the waka enigma away from the rigid, conventional ideas taught in our schools and academies—ideas that are increasingly being questioned today.

Without physical evidence, or an oral or written record by the people who created these wakas,* we are left with vague interpretations as to their origins and original purpose. However, it's clear that they were built by people who tracked the movement of the stars, worshipped the elements, and connected with the spiritual world—especially when it comes to the Hanan Pacha work. Still, I suggest

---

*Although there are reports from Spanish Chroniclers that Inca Pachacuti created Sacsayhuaman and Ollantaytambo, it is unclear if they were talking about the massive megalithic work or more conventional Inca work that is found at the site. I believe it is the latter based on the four reasons stated above.

there might be something even more enigmatic to the waka question, something that could take us much further back in time to when they were created.

## A SCIENTIFIC AND ESOTERIC APPROACH

In this book, I explore some of the more recent scientific discoveries that can help us shine light on how the megaliths and monoliths were built, and examine some of the possible uses for the wakas. I will also explore the Gamarras' Cosmogony of the Three Worlds, which is based on the expanding Earth and three orbits theories and their correspondence with the three distinct time periods associated with human development. I will also delve into the esoteric examinations of Rudolf Steiner, Madame Blavatsky, Edgar Cayce, and Satguru Sivaya Subramuniya, plus their insights about the ancient past via their penetration into the Akashic Records (a nonphysical plane of existence where all events, thoughts, words, and intentions are encoded into the fabric of space), which are mainly complementary to Gamarra's theories.

So why use esotericists like Steiner, Cayce, Blavatsky, and the Hindu mystic Subramuniya to gather perception into these early worlds? Well, mainly because of the nature of the subject matter—understanding what humans were like before there was a written record in the ancient past. Without having a time machine to see into the past, it is compelling to explore alternative methods, like those communicated by clairvoyants and psychics. I also selected the specific above-mentioned individuals for their highly respected position in the world of esoteric sciences. If one is to take Rudolf Steiner at his word, the world seen in the Akashic Records is much more accurate than what can be gleaned from the dusty, and sometimes deceptive, documents in the external sense world. He writes:

People who have acquired the ability to perceive in the spiritual world come to know past events in their eternal character. Such events do not stand before them like the dead testimony of history, but appear in full life. It is almost as if what has happened takes place before them. Those initiated into the reading of such a living script can look back into a much more remote past than is represented by external history, and—on the basis of direct spiritual perception—they can also describe much more reliably the things of which history tells.[3]

One of the key concepts that makes the revelations of Steiner, Blavatsky, Cayce, and Subramuniya so intriguing is that they all say that early humans were of a different constitution in body, mind, and spirit than that of contemporary peoples—one that was more ethereal in nature in the beginning, but over time evolved into a more material body as their third-dimensional senses and organs evolved. In earlier evolution, humans were said not only to be more attuned to their environment, but also could master the subtle energies within it; they knew how to mold rock, harness the energy in seeds, and co-create life.

If these earlier humans were the creators of this first style of construction, this might explain why some of the most sacred and revered places on Earth are built right on what appear to be Hanan Pacha rocks, with one of the most famous examples located at the Temple Mount in Jerusalem, below the Islamic shrine known as the Dome of the Rock. From *Smithsonian Magazine*, we get an eye-widening description of the significance of this stone:

The Dome of the Rock is built on top of the Foundation Stone, which is sacred to both Jews and Muslims. According to Jewish tradition, the stone is the "navel of the Earth"—the place where creation began, and the site where Abraham was poised to sacrifice Isaac. For Muslims, the stone marks the place where the Prophet Muhammad ascended to the Divine Presence.[4]

And, from the Jewish book *Zohar*, we read about this rock:

The world was not created until God took a stone called *Even haShetiya* and threw it into the depths where it was fixed from above till below, and from it the world expanded. It is the center point of the world and on this spot stood the Holy of Holies.[5]

The Foundation Stone seems to be part of the ninety-million-year-old karsted limestone from the Upper Turonian Stage, Late Cretaceous.[6] Can this account about the Foundation Stone's age be our first indicator of a timeline associated with the first humans on Earth, or were the strange forms on it inscribed much later?

This is an interesting bit of information in light of Steiner's and Blavatsky's theories of when the first solidified humans were alleged to have materialized, in the late Lemurian and early Atlantean periods. The *Zohar* also mentions an expanding Earth, which is interesting in light of the Gamarras' assertions.

Some have claimed that the carvings found on the Foundation Stone were made by the Crusaders, who were hunting treasure at the Temple Mount, though other critics dispute this, for good reason. Most likely, if the Crusaders were seeking treasure they would dig around and under the stone—not through it. And if they wanted to put their mark on this stone, we would see more classic Christian iconography from the time, such as a cross, but there is no evidence of religious iconography or writing upon it.

If we look at the 1859 watercolor of the Foundation Stone by Carl Haag (fig. i.8), it demonstrates the abstract nature of the shapes on top of the rock quite clearly—shapes that we can see in other Hanan Pacha sites from all around the world. I feel when gazing at the painting that I am looking at many of the wakas in Cusco, as they are so similar with their strange nobs, niches, and indents.

I understand that this book presents many ideas out of the mainstream and may not interest many readers who prefer to get their

Fig. i.8. "The Foundation Stone" by Carl Haag.
See also color plate 4.

Fig. i.9. Waka Ñusta Tianan opposite
Waka Cheqtaqaqa, Cusco, Peru.

answers about history from more "authoritative" sources. But if you are one of the few who does question the dominant narratives, it is my sincerest hope that this book helps you gain insights about our ancient past.

This study is purely speculative, based on my personal research and intuition. Please take what resonates with you and leave behind what doesn't.

I hope you enjoy the journey.

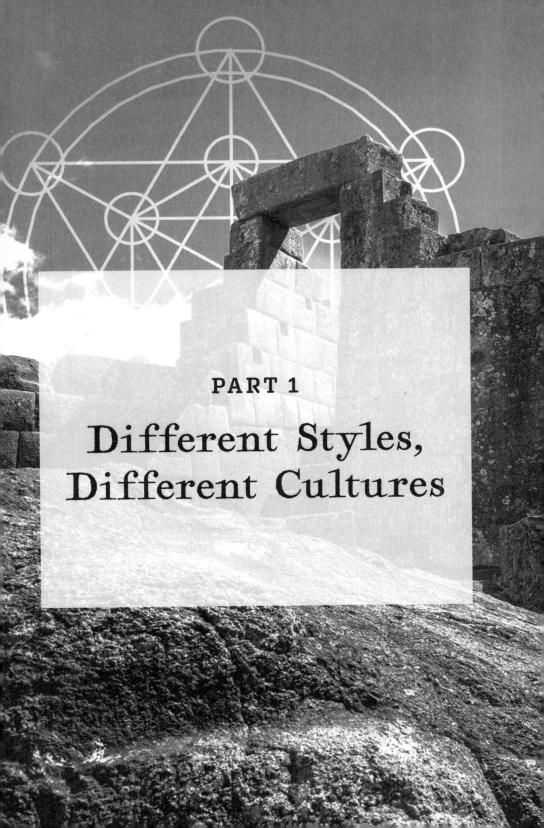

# PART 1
# Different Styles,
# Different Cultures

# 1

# The Cosmogony of the Three Worlds

*Wonder at the things that are before you,*
*making this the first step to further knowledge.*

JESUS, FROM APOCRYPHAL GOSPEL OF MATTHIAS

C usco city and the wider Cusco province of Peru make up a stunningly beautiful region. Giant mist-covered mountains (known as *apus* in the Quechua language) surround you in all directions, and the gleaming waters of the Urubamba and Acomayo Rivers snake their way through some of the most striking valley scenery. Rainbows materialize frequently as if a sign from Inti (the Andean sun god) to remind you of the sacredness of his light and the elements. You feel the land's enchantment here as well as its mystery, and it is not just imagined.

As you walk through Cusco's old town you literally pass through a pastiche of ancient structures left over from the Inca, Killke, and other cultures—some possibly older than we can imagine. The patchwork of multicolored rock walls—some made with rough misshapen stones, others polygonal and perfectly fitted to their adjacent mates—whisper to you to look at them, and you willingly comply. Sometimes you feel the need to touch them as you hope that they may impart their mysteries to you through osmosis, but mainly you do so because they are irresistible—you need to caress their textured skin and shiny edges, and feel their radiating heat, as if you've found your long-lost lover.

It is because of this love of stone, and the rich culture here, that I have made Cusco and the Sacred Valley my home. Nothing makes me happier than to explore the ancient sites in Cusco, as well as the surrounding areas in the Valley, for the mysterious and magical wakas, (sometimes spelled *huacas*), or sacred sites, that dot the landscape in the hundreds. In particular, I like to examine the sites most tourists and travelers never get to see because they are off the main circuits, ones you can examine in a leisurely fashion without the crowds. Another added benefit is they are free and frequently unguarded by security, so you can spend more time exploring them, and sometimes get into areas that are ostensibly off limits.

Some of my favorite areas in the Sacsayhuaman complex are Amaru Marca Wasi, also called the Temple de la Luna (Moon Temple) and K'usilluchayoq (Monkey Temple), both on the Inca Road headed to Cusco city, as well as Q'enko Chico (Little Labyrinth), which is below his big brother, Q'enko (Labyrinth). I also have made frequent visits to the majestic Grand Chincana, and to the mysterious and somewhat dangerous "Zone X,"* as well as to the various wakas in the residential areas of upper Cusco.

All of these sites have unique features that make them stand out from other building styles that we see in later cultures in the area. They are monoliths, meaning that they are made from a single, usually massive rock, typically of hardened limestone. They frequently feature strange and sometimes incongruent forms like rough, mountain-like peaks with deep depressions next to perfectly molded *sillas* (chairs or thrones), basins, and niches. Many

---

*I have personally heard stories of people getting mugged there, as well as people getting injured while exploring the caves.

are whimsical and organic and others show forms of animals like snakes, cats, and monkeys (although heavily damaged from time and the destructive purges of sacred sites by the Spanish). They are often near or sit directly on top of water sources.

Fig. 1.1. Hanan Pacha forms at Little Q'enko, Sacsayhuaman.
See also color plate 5.

They also show signs that they were venerated by later people to such a degree that these later cultures built massive walls around them as a sign of their sacredness (see fig. 1.3 p. 19). You can view this clearly at the main complex of Sacsayhuaman, Tambomachay, Puma Pukara, and at Q'enko Chico, as well as many other sites in the Sacsayhuaman Park. In even more recent times, you can see Killke or Incan dwellings (see fig. 1.4 p. 20) near or even right on top of them. This is a common sight in Peru; you can find evidence of this veneration of the older style all throughout the country.

Even though the dissimilar-looking structures appear as if they were built by completely different cultures, the official guides and

Fig. 1.2. Images of a snake and monkey at the Monkey Temple.
Photo by Francisco Carbajal.

Fig.1.3. Inca construction in the northern part of Sacsayhuaman Park.
See also color plate 6.

Fig. 1.4. Uran Pacha polygonal stones surround
Colina Suchuna, a Hanan Pacha site.
See also color plate 7.

archaeologists that I met were almost unanimous in their pronounce-
ments that the Inca built every structure in the park. But to me, this
seems irrational and overly simplistic. For instance, why would the Inca
build such complicated, not to mention massively time-consuming to
construct, polygonal walls around a monolithic stone waka that they
themselves built earlier? And why the different styles? Even the best-
selling author and researcher of ancient mysteries, Graham Hancock,
says that it is only in Peru that archaeologists ignore obviously different styles of construction for fear of going against the established
theory that the Inca built them. He writes:

> In the absence of useful objective tests [to gauge a stone's age], there-
> fore, the next strategy is to look at architectural style and methods.
> Just as different styles of pottery can often provide reliable indica-
> tions as to what culture in what period made a particular piece, so
> too with architecture. The rule of thumb is that very different styles

and approaches to the construction or creation of stone monuments, even if they are side by side, are indicative of the involvement of different cultures working at different periods in the past.[1]

This seems like a very reasonable conclusion, and because it is part of established archaeology practice in every part of the world, why not use this approach to understand what is going on in Peru?

Equally problematic to me is that we have two highly dubious accounts—repeated unquestioningly over countless travel and government websites—about who actually built the giant megalithic walls of the citadel of Sacsayhuaman. The more commonly heard narrative is that they were built by the ninth Inca king Pachecutec who was said to have employed a massive workforce of tens of thousands of workers who not only transported the massive limestone rocks from the quarry over four kilometers away, but also shaped the massive stones to a perfect-fitting, jigsaw-puzzle perfection with their simple rock and bronze and copper tools.[2]

The other popular narrative is that the Killke built the megalithic walls and the Inca later expanded on them. Amazingly, if you type "Killke culture buildings" in Google, the first thing that comes up are the massive megalithic walls at Sacsayhuaman; however, they don't look anything like the known Killke sites excavated by archaeologists.

As Fernando Astete, director of Machu Picchu Archaeological Park, points out, Killke architecture "is characterized by its resemblance to the Inca, however the latter stands out for its very well defined, geometric structures, with a very good finish" and "[on] the other hand, the Killke does not have that geometry nor does it have a good finish, it is much more rustic . . . ."[3] An example of Killke construction is seen in figure 1.5 (p. 22), and one can easily make out that it looks nothing like the citadel walls at Sacsayhuaman.

These two bizarre creation myths for Sacsayhuaman seem to be the only ones deemed reputable by mainstream academics today. However, there is an ever-growing chorus of skeptics that claim the site shows

Fig. 1.5. Known Killke site in Machu Picchu.
Public domain.

evidence of advanced technology—like molded rock forms, vitrification, perfect drill holes, and the ability to lift incredibly heavy stones and fit them into puzzle-perfect forms—that should preclude these cultures as the creators. For my part, as well as these skeptics, the official story hasn't adequately given us a believable answer as to how a Bronze Age culture like the Inca or Killke could have made these structures.

## THE HERETICS

In my many excursions around Peru, I have discovered quite a few Indigenous people, some who are given the duty of watching over sites for the Ministry of Culture, who break the taboo and say these sites are not only pre-Inca and very ancient but that no one seems to know when they were built. According to some, these sites existed "before their ancestors were around."

I even met a few *paco* (shaman) types on the Sacsayhuaman grounds who gave a much less standard interpretation of the site, which I found refreshing. A couple of them said that the wakas were created by star beings and others said that they were built by a very ancient civilization, mimicking statements made by Indigenous Quechua-speaking attendants working for the Ministry of Culture. Since most of them and their ancestors have lived in the area for many generations, if not thousands of years, maybe we should assume that they might know something about who created these sites—or, more specifically, who did not.

I find it disturbing that so many archaeologists don't give these Indigenous stories much, if any, credibility. Unfortunately, this is the case with so many other Indigenous societies, whose beliefs and oral traditions get ignored by mainstream archaeologists (except those by Spanish Chroniclers or the royal descendants of the Inca). This is a stagnant and soulless approach that, in my opinion, needs to be examined seriously by historians and archaeologists, as it is very likely that we will have a skewed and probably erroneous account of history without these stories.

Besides the accounts of many Indigenous people, there are independent researchers that have questioned the official proclamations of orthodox history and archaeology, and have discovered that officialdom hates to have its applecart shaken. Graham Hancock, who has been a recipient of much criticism and ridicule for thinking outside the circumscribed historical box—along with other alternative researchers and historians into prehistory—has repeatedly said that the discipline of archaeology is a very conservative and rigid field, with archaeologists being averse to questioning anything their peers and predecessors have already pronounced as true. We can also assume that many archaeologists, teachers, and historians believe that their careers will be jeopardized if they deviate from the path of orthodox belief, so they obediently toe the line.

Fortunately, there are a few brave souls in academia who have come out against the academic protocols that are designed to make historical analysis of sites a closed-loop system. For instance, Andean scholar Dr. Albert Meyers, former research associate at the Department of Ancient American Studies at the University of Bonn, has spoken out publicly and critically of the methodology used by many of his colleagues to assign dates to archaeology sites. In his paper, "Inca Archaeology and The Late Horizon: Some Polemic Remarks," he writes of the overreliance by Andean historians and archaeologists on ethnohistorical material as the basis of determining an archaeological site's age:

> We know much more about the Inka than before, much more details about their material culture and its spread over a vast territory of the Andes. Yet on the other hand, for some crucial aspects of this culture, its origin and expansion we are still confronted with unproved hypotheses and generalizations, eclecticisms and the simple repetition of popular myths. . . . The principal bias still consists in the unconditional application of "historically derived" interpretations of the archaeological context. The critical point is there that archaeologists after presenting their evidences draw the conclusions by fitting the material to the historic model or look for an archaeological verification of the historical interpretation . . . .[4]

Another scholar of pre-Columbian history, the ethnologist and archaeologist Walter Krickeberg, also describes how relying solely on historical accounts can distort a true understanding of history. Here he provides an example of how even one of the most respected chroniclers, Garcilaso de la Vega, who was of mixed Spanish and Inca ancestry, tended to assign significant institutions to his ancestors, the Inca—when, in fact, the Inca assimilated systems from many other cultures:

> For a very long time, no doubt was cast on the statements of the chronicler Garcilaso de la Vega, descended from the Incas, who

attributed to the Incas all sorts of institutions which in reality were anterior to the Incas and merely incorporated, unchanged by them, into their system of government, with practical common sense, and an acute awareness of political expediency.[5]

Could we be seeing a similar inclination to ascribe the hundreds of wakas in the Cusco environs to the Inca or Killke to fit the dominant historical narrative—narratives that seem a bit too heavily weighted in their recognition that the last known major cultures in the region were the progenitors of major archaeology sites? Is this what is going on when chroniclers assert that sites such as Sacsayhuaman and Machu Picchu were wholly Inca (or Inca/Killke) built? Here Dr. Meyers relays his doubts about their origins:

Archaeological sites and architectural units are treated as related to known Inca kings or groups and in their functions as described by the 16th century documents, but archaeologically spoken there nothing is clear, neither in terms of chronology nor of a cultural transition from early Inca to Imperial Inca.

Meyer recommends that archaeologists should consider analyzing archaeology sites independently of historical documents:

Another procedure could be to simply accept this and start with a completely different approach and of course methodology, define the archaeological context, analyze it with its own methods and draw the conclusion separately from the historical studies and interpretations?[6]

What Meyers recommends is certainly more sensible and scientific than just taking the hearsay of chroniclers that may have some ulterior motive in assigning monumental works to the most contemporary culture of the day. History is often distorted based on the chroniclers'

Fig. 1.6. The author in front of a giant polygonal
wall at Sacsayhuaman. See also color plate 3.

prejudices or assumptions—like the belief that since the Inca were
known to have built structures at or near Sacsayhuaman and at other
major sites, then they must have created all the structures on the site.
This is a questionable conclusion if ever there was one.

Although it is important to also reference historical documents,
the physical, empirical evidence should also weigh as important, if not
more so, when trying to figure out who built these sites. Maybe, if we
applied some of the methodology that Meyers suggests—along with
other interdisciplinary approaches, like geological fieldwork—we could
at least establish a timeframe as to when these wakas were really built.

One thing I discovered in my walks around Sacsayhuaman is that
many wakas are buried under tons of layers of sediment. In some
places I have seen them covered in more than two meters of soil. A
Peruvian friend (who also tends to back the official story that the
Incas constructed all the work around Sacsayhuaman) told me that

he has seen sites buried much deeper than this. This begs the question: how did so much sediment accumulate in so little time when the Incas, or their immediate predecessors the Killke (900 to 1200 CE), were alleged to have created these sites, 600 to 1,100 years ago respectively? It is particularly mysterious since most of these sites are on high ground without many mountains around them. Just where did the soil come from?

If there were massive flooding events in the last thousand years or so—events of such proportions as to bury these monuments under vast amounts of soil—it would seem likely that historians or oral histories from people living in the Andes would have recorded them. But in my research, I have found no such stories. Also, if such an event did happen, the mudflow would go straight into the city of Cusco, which is a bowl-shaped depression right below the steep hill of the Sacsayhuaman complex. One can see that Sacsayhuaman has a lot of ravines, both natural and man-made, to direct water and sediment off the mountain and into the city. So again, how did the sites get so deeply buried?

## GOING OFF THE DEEP END

Trying to make sense of this puzzle, I started doing research into what others were saying about the different types of building styles. I eventually found the web page of Jan Peter de Jong, who, like me, had doubts as to the official story. He writes:

> Until I came in contact with Jesús Gamarra, the son of the late Alfredo Gamarra, I had not realized myself how far off current science might be. Jesús showed me phenomena in the ruins in and around Cusco, Peru. The official view is that everything in the ruins was created by the Inca. There are stunning buildings, made with great precision and often [of] gigantic dimensions, in fantastic beautiful locations. One who sees these ruins for the first time is

impressed by them, as I was. One thinks, this is very cleverly done by the Inca, but most will think that there is not much more to say about those old stones.

However, fate willed that I moved to live in Cusco. Because of daily contact with the ruins, such as the famous perfect fitting walls, and by working together with Jesús Gamarra, I began to see things in a new light. One stone is not the same as the others. Jesús told me about the precision, the giant dimensions, the different styles, the phenomenon of "vitrification," etc . . . . All of this is repeated in other ruins, in the same way and in the same order, from Cusco to Sacsayhuaman, from the Sacred Valley of the Inca to Machu Picchu. Eventually, it is repeated on the global level; we can see the same phenomena in Egypt.

We learn more about Alfredo Gamarra's Cosmogony of the Three Worlds in this excerpt from de Jong:

In the first world, called Hanan Pacha or "Heaven above," people could live almost eternally and had more capacities than we, especially mentally speaking. Humanity did not know fatigue, the stature of man was about 4m.20, man was able to fly without having wings, all this, said Alfredo, because of the small amount of gravity. Man was also able to amass stone and used a molding technology, under high temperatures. Nowadays this can be recognized in monolithic structures, in which vitrification is present. In this time the anatomic structure of the human being was cartilaginous, as a result of the smaller atmospheric pressure. Alfredo Gamarra related this time to the first and underlying construction style of many sacred monuments all over the world, as in the Great Pyramid, Malta, Stonehenge, and the Temple Mount. The location where this construction style exists relatively more, is near his own hometown Cusco, Peru, in the vestiges that are normally considered as Inca. For Alfredo it was the major reason to think that

Cusco, not only for the Incas, but also in very ancient times, really was the navel of the world. [7]

The first style, *Hanan Pacha*, is what Gamarra believed was the oldest style, and constitutes the collection of sites that are monolithic and abstract in nature. They are not only found in Peru but all over the world and seem to be revered as sacred by the civilizations that came after it. The second style, *Uran Pacha* (land of the heaven below), features walls that use perfectly fitted stones usually of a megalithic (or large stone) nature and with no mortar. This type of construction is seen on the main complex walls at Sacsayhuaman, as well as at other sites with polygonal stone work in Peru and around the world. The last style, *Ukun Pacha* (land of the heaven inside), refers to more recent styles, ones that encompass the Killke, Wari, and Incan civilizations in Peru, and which have a building style of using smaller, loose-fitting stones, often with mortar between the rocks.

Gamarra's theory tied these styles to the expanding Earth theory and his belief that the Earth was at different orbits during different periods of its creation. He said that these early orbits and the smaller size of the planet had produced a much less dense world due to less gravity, making it easier for early humans to manipulate physical elements in their environment.

According to de Jong, Alfredo Gamarra didn't actually mention an expanding earth in discussions with his son, Jesús. However, Gamarra Sr. did believe that at one time in our geological history the Earth was smaller. When de Jong and Jesús were discussing this smaller Earth theory on an online forum on Graham Hancock's website, some of the readers brought up the expanding earth hypothesis, and, later de Jong added this theory on his website as a possible explanation for why the Earth was at one time smaller than it is today, which would be a logical conclusion.

Listed on the next page, Jan Peter de Jong sums up Alfredo Gamarra's main theories on his website. Here is his list of the most important and controversial conclusions:

Fig. 1.7. The three worlds and their orbits.
Courtesy of Jesús Gamarra and Jan Peter de Jong.

- Earth was smaller in the past.
- Earth went through different periods corresponding to different orbits of Earth around the sun, with, of course, different calendars.
- Life was bigger in the past thanks to less gravity.
- Humanity could live longer thanks to less gravity.
- Monolithic and megalithic constructions were easier to construct thanks to less gravity.
- Construction of these monuments was done with moldable stones.
- The precision of the perfect fitting stones was thanks to the stones being moldable at the moment of construction.
- The vestiges of Cusco and surroundings are much older than "Inca time."[8]

De Jong, who has collaborated with Alfredo's son, Jesús, on championing "The Cosmology of the Three Worlds" on his website, and via a video of the same name, also adds his own theories on how early humans were able to affect their environment. One of them was that early humans could access "the field" more easily because there was less gravity. Here he writes:

> My interpretation, based on the way of thinking of Alfredo Gamarra, is the following: presently, due to a world with more gravity and more density of all the materials, it is more difficult for us to have access to the "Field." With the Field I mean the term used by Lynne McTaggart in her book with the same name, and featured in Dan Brown's . . . *The Lost Symbol*: Human consciousness, as Noetic author Lynne McTaggart described it, was a substance outside the confines of the body. A highly ordered energy capable of changing the physical world. The Field in this sense is "the interconnected universe," where everything and everyone is connected.

De Jong states on his website that people in the far past could connect to this Field because with less gravity and atmospheric density, it was easier for this early humanity to do so. As a consequence of these conditions, people had more telepathic powers, so they had easier access to common knowledge—not only of other people, but other life forms and energies in the Field—and thus more "immediate results of intention were possible."[9]

De Jong's hypothesis seems to align with Alfredo Gamarra's theory that early humans had a strong intuitive understanding of their world, as well as psychic abilities that could easily shape their environment.

If the Gamarras' and de Jong's hypotheses that the world was much smaller and less dense are true, it seems like they are truly going out to the final frontier of acceptable timelines, because we are talking about a human history that is not thousands of years old, or tens of thousands, but millions if not tens of millions years old!

Fig. 1.8. Alfredo Gamarra with Sacsayhuaman in the background.
Courtesy of Jesús Gamarra and Jan Peter de Jong.

If the standard, conventional view of academics is that humanity evolved from a primitive ape-like creature called *Australopithecus afarensis*, with a small brain and stature, about 3.5 million years ago—and that modern humans (*Homo sapiens sapiens*) only came on the scene some 100,000 years ago—then the theory that humans in the far more distant past were so advanced is beyond the pale of consensus science. Could this be even remotely possible?

I can't discount this radical theory out of hand. I have spent so much time examining the Hanan and Uran Pacha monuments around Sacsayhuaman, and in other areas around the Andes, to realize that they do look like they were made by the mind of a very different kind of being.

The Gamarras' and de Jong's theories also vaguely call to mind the works of Rudolf Steiner, with which I have some familiarity, as I have spent many years, off and on, reading his books and listening to his lectures about the evolution of humanity. His book *Atlantis and*

*Lemuria* contains some surprising similarities to the Gamarras' theories, ones that may boost the idea that humanity may have been around for much, much longer than conventional archaeologists and historians would dare to acknowledge, or even speculate.

■ ■ ■

In the next chapter we will explore the expanding Earth and closer orbit theories and see if there is any scientific weight to these concepts.

# 2

# The Expanding
# Earth Timeline

*Then Yima stepped forward, towards the luminous space,
southwards, to meet the sun, and pressed the earth with the
golden ring, and bored it with the poniard, speaking thus:
"O Earth, kindly open asunder and stretch thyself afar,
to bear flocks and herds and men." And Yima made the
Earth grow larger by three-thirds than it was before, and
there came flocks and herds and men, at his will and wish,
as many as he wished.*

ZEND-AVESTA, VENDIDAD,
FARGARD II, VERSES 18–19

Jan Peter de Jong and Jesús Gamarra indicate that the earth may
have grown in mass over eons and eons of time, and, this idea
would fit into the proposition by Alfredo Gamarra that the Earth was
at on one time 55% smaller and had less gravity. My first reaction when
I read about this theory was that if this were true, then we must be talking about events that could have only taken place tens of millions years
ago, if not hundreds of millions of years ago. Could it be possible that

some type of early human was around such an impossibly long time ago to create Hanan Pacha work?

I decided to examine the expanding Earth theory to see what the scientific community was saying about this. I was quite surprised to find there is a lot of support for the expanding Earth theory among quite a few modern and historical famous scientists—including Charles Darwin, Isaac Newton, and Nikola Tesla!

In an article by Sandra Herbert—"Charles Darwin as a Prospective Geological Author," written for the *British Journal for the History of Science*—the author mentions that in 1834, during the second voyage of the HMS *Beagle*, Charles Darwin investigated stepped plains featuring raised beaches in Patagonia, which indicated to him that a huge area of South America had been "uplifted to its present height by a succession of elevations which acted over the whole of this space with nearly an equal force." Herbert goes on to say that Darwin believed that this uplift was due to the gradual expansion of the central mass of the Earth "acting by intervals on the outer crust."

The equally as famous Serbian American inventor Nikola Tesla wrote in a 1935 op-ed in *The New York Herald Tribune* that:

> Condensation of the primary substance is going on continuously, this being in a measure proved, for I have established by experiments which admit of no doubt that the sun and other celestial bodies steadily increase in mass and energy and ultimately must explode, reverting to the primary substance.[2]

Was Tesla only speaking of suns here or all celestial bodies, which would include the planets? It is unclear. What is clear though is that Tesla and other leading scientists of the day, like Osipovich Yarkovsky,[3] were proponents of the theory that matter can be created out of aether energy.

It turns out that another luminary in science, Issac Newton, also

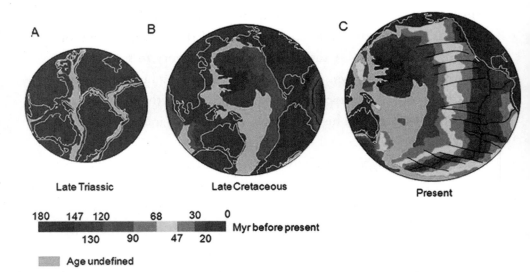

Fig. 2.1. Planetary expansion from Late Triassic, Late Cretaceous to present day according to Dennis McCarthy.

suggested such an aether medium existed in the universe, in his book *The Third Book of Opticks.* In it he wrote:

> Doth not this aethereal medium in passing out of water, glass, crystal, and other compact and dense bodies in empty spaces, grow denser and denser by degrees, and by that means refract the rays of light not in a point, but by bending them gradually in curve lines? . . . Is not this medium much rarer within the dense bodies of the Sun, stars, planets and comets, than in the empty celestial space between them? And in passing from them to great distances, doth it not grow denser and denser perpetually, and thereby cause the gravity of those great bodies towards one another, and of their parts towards the bodies; every body endeavoring to go from the denser parts of the medium towards the rarer?[4]

Although *aether energy* sounds very exotic and is a term generally heard in spiritual traditions, today it has a more general meaning of a field in space, or a medium for the propagation of electromagnetic and gravitational forces. It is frequently called the quantum field, or more simply the Field. Although the Field is not fully understood by the scientific community, or many of its concepts accepted, this Field could explain how planets and celestial bodies can grow.

I found an interesting paper online by David Noel (from the Ben Franklin Centre for Theoretical Research, based in Subiaco, Australia) titled "Continental Drift And Earth Expansion." Noel seemed to have a logical explanation of geological time based on the expanding Earth model, which also matches forensic rock dating. He writes:

> The basis of the Expanding Earth proposition is that the current continental masses were once all joined completely together, covering the whole surface of a much smaller Earth. This has since expanded internally, the current continents splitting apart and distributing themselves over the enlarged surface. In other words, the current deep-sea areas did not exist in their present conformation in earlier times, but have been formed by the expansion of the Earth's core under them.
>
> At present, about 70% of the Earth's surface is covered by sea. If the present 30% surface, which is land, had to cover the whole of a smaller sphere, that sphere would be about 55% of the diameter of the present Earth. Instead of the current radius of about 6,400 km, the radius would have been around 3,500 km. The circumference of the present Earth is 40,000 km, but an "unexpanded" Earth, in which Pangaea covered the whole surface, would have a circumference of about 22,000 km, that is, 18,000 km less than now.
>
> It is interesting to calculate how long this expansion would have taken, at the present rate observed in sea-floor spreading. Since the rate at each ridge is around 2–4 cm/yr, and there are usually 3 ridges crossed in going right round the Earth, the total present expansion is very roughly 9 cm/yr. Dividing this into 18,000 km gives an expansion time of 200 my [million years ago], which agrees quite well with the time from rock age-dating.[5]

If this is true—that the Earth has been expanding, and is continuing to expand today—it may also explain the decrease of gravity that the Gamarras and de Jong have put forth in their Three Worlds Cosmogony. If Earth were 55 percent smaller, it would have less gravity because of its smaller mass. This could explain why animals and humans were much larger in the past, as their bodies had less pull on them from the Earth's gravity.

So, some things I hadn't quite understood about the Gamarras' theory are now beginning to make a bit more sense for me—except for the early humanity part, which is still problematic for me, because I don't have any physical evidence to reference that shows that humanity has existed for such a long period of time.

Since I couldn't find anything online by the Gamarras that referenced the timeframe of when this early humanity was supposed to exist, I decided I needed to meet with Alfredo Gamarra's son, Jesús, in person, to get some clarity about this issue.

I met Jesús Gamarra in his home near the San Pedro market area in Cusco on March 23, 2022. As we entered Jesús's personal office, we encountered a large collection of pan flutes and other instruments that looked very old. Jesús is a musician and played with his band, the GAGS, in Cusco for many decades. He showed me a lovely two-color poster he designed for his band. Prominently featured on the poster was the famous *Intihuatana* (hitching post) from Machu Picchu, a fitting graphic for one who loves the history of Peru so much.

Jesús, like anyone who is really enthralled with a topic, got very animated when talking about the subject of wakas, and for more than two hours the spritely, slightly Spock-looking seventy-seven-year-old came alive while discussing his and his father's theories. Holding his personal book *Parawayso* (Quechua for "Paradise") in hand, Jesús went over almost chapter by chapter some of the key concepts outlined in the book. Some of them I knew already, but many I didn't—like his belief that ancient biblical texts describe the land of Cus (Cusco) to be the center of the world and the first Eden, and that there was a pre-

Columbian map drawn by Ptolemy that shows the coast of Peru very clearly.

I bought his book to explore these theories in the future. However, the main reasons I was there—besides wanting to meet a legend in speculative history—was because I was trying to make sense of the timeframes for which the three worlds were alleged to exist.

When I asked him, "When do you think the Hanan Pacha period was in Earth's history?" I unfortunately got an answer that was even more unrealistic than the 200 million years quoted above: Jesús said that the beginning of the Hanan Pacha monoliths started around 100,000 years ago! My first thought was that this might make sense if one looked at the Hanan Pacha timeframe from a conventional archaeological perspective on an unexpanded Earth—but how could this timeframe match up with a much smaller Earth that was significantly closer to the sun?

Unfortunately, since my Spanish is just basic, and Jesús's English is similarly limited, I asked my partner, Francisco, who is a native speaker, to ask Jesús for clarification, and to convey the idea that scientists believe Pangaea existed at a much earlier period in Earth's history, closer to 200 million years ago. However, once again, I was given the same number—100,000 years—without an explanation as to how he had determined it.

I knew that the Gamarras' Three Worlds theory is based on the premise that there were early humans able to manipulate their environment due to there being less gravity during the Hanan Pacha and Uran Pacha times—because as they theorized, the Earth was smaller and had less mass. I don't have any issue with this premise in general, as there were many scientists in the past, and are scientists today, who do believe in the expanding Earth theory—plus, it seems very plausible looking at how the continents seem to fit together like in a puzzle. However, if this smaller Earth theory were to be true we would have to push the timeline back considerably, as I am sure there was hardly any difference in Earth's size 100,000 years ago.

It is estimated that our Earth is 4.5 billion years old, so 100,000 years is just a rounding error in geological terms. Also, as I stated above, the time when this Earth was small enough to have all the continents touching each other would have been around 200 million years ago, when there existed the supercontinent Pangaea. So even though I think there may be something to the expanding Earth theory, unfortunately Gamarra's timeline, or at least his son Jesús theory of Hanan Pacha work, doesn't mesh with Earth geological time.

In the next chapter we will look into the Three Worlds, Three Orbits theory of the Gamarras.

■ ■ ■

Shortly before this book was ready for press, I had a follow up discussion with de Jong regarding Jesús Gamarra's take on the expanding earth theory, varying Earth orbits, and the possible timelines assigned to these events. De Jong told me, that Jesús Gamarra believed that there probably have been more orbit changes, [but] only the last 3 are with human life. De Jong also relayed that Jesús believed that the last big Ice Ages were the result of an orbit change, and that he didn't believe that the first orbit change was when the continents were together 200 million years ago. De Jong said that he was the one more partial to expanding earth theory as it worked well with Sr. Gamarra's smaller Earth theory. He also said that to assign dating methodologies to Earth's history is problematic for these reasons: "They are based on the assumption of a stable earth, and exactly this is not true within the expanding earth theory and Gamarra's theory, circumstances of mass, gravity, air pressure etc, were very different [over time]."

# 3

# Three Worlds,
# Three Orbits?

Alfredo Gamarra believed that the three distinctive styles of building (Hanan Pacha, Uran Pacha, and Ukun Pacha) are related to a time when Earth had distinctive orbits around the sun. It was during these epochs in history that humans had distinctive physical characteristics and abilities that distinguished them from the other worlds.

As mentioned in earlier chapters, Hanan Pacha was the first period of time, and according to Gamarra, it was a time when the Earth was supposed to be the closest to the sun and had an orbit of 225 days. In this world, gravity was considerably weaker and the human constitution was more ethereal. Humans were instinctively masters of the elements in nature and could manipulate their environment with ease.

During Uran Pacha, the middle period of time, the Earth had an orbit of 260 days, and it was located approximately half the distance between the Earth's orbit today and the Hanan Pacha orbit. Its gravity was also weaker, but not as pronounced as Hanan Pacha times. The Earth's surface began to expand, but was not near the size of our present Earth. During this period it was thought that giants were on the Earth.

Ukun Pacha is the present day, or the relatively recent period of time. This epoch would include buildings built by the Inca, Killke, or Wari, and other more recent cultures in Peru. It is the time when the Earth has come to its full, present-day size and reached a 365-day orbit.

If we discount our contemporary 365-day orbit, what evidence do we have that the Earth might have had two distinct orbits in the past? I could not find much in the scientific or historical literature about such a notion, but I did find an article titled "Earth Is Drifting Away From The Sun, And So Are All The Planets," by Forbes senior science contributor, Ethan Siegel. He states:

> Earth's orbital path doesn't remain the same over time, but spirals outward. This year, 2019, our perihelion was 1.5 centimeters farther away than it was last year, which was more distant than the year before, etc. It's not just Earth, either; every planet drifts away from its parent star . . .
>
> The Sun's mass loss, by burning its nuclear fuel, ensures that every mass orbiting in our Solar System is slowly spiraling outward as time goes on. Some 4.5 billion years ago, our planet was around 50,000 kilometers closer to the Sun than it is today, and will grow more distant more rapidly as the Sun continues to evolve.
>
> With each and every orbit that passes, the planets become progressively less tightly-bound to our Sun. The rate at which the Sun burns through its fuel is increasing, accelerating the rate at which all the planets spiral outwards. While this should never unbind any of the planets we have today, the slow, steady, outward migration of every world is inevitable.

Siegel explains that we are pulling away from our central star due to nuclear fusion, the process by which the sun takes the mass at the core of its body and converts it into energy. Over time, according to Siegel, this conversion of matter into energy results in the sun losing a considerable amount of mass.

On a year-by-year basis, the Sun loses some 4.7 million tons of matter, which lessens the gravitational pull on every object in our Solar System. It's this gravitational pull that causes our orbits to behave as we know them to behave.[1]

Does this description explain why Earth—and all the planets—are moving away from our parent star and why there would have been different orbits in the past? I guess if we look at it from the perspective of a gradual pulling away of the Earth over vast periods of time it does, but it doesn't explain a significant orbital jump as Gamarra's Three World Orbits would seem to imply. If we look at Siegel's calculations, the numbers are almost negligible as far as the distance the Earth's orbit has moved from the sun since its inception. For example, if we conclude that this theory is correct, it would mean that in 4.5 billion years the Earth has only moved 50,000 kilometers, or just 31,070 miles away from the sun. Today we know the Earth is 150 million kilometers, or 93 million miles away from the sun, so this shouldn't have any significant effect on overall gravity or relative distance of the Earth to the sun.

Also, what Siegel is explaining here is known as Milankovitch Cycles, named after the Serbian mathematician, climatologist, and geophysicist Milutin Milankovitch, who calculated how the orbit of the Earth goes through a recurring hanging orbit that fluctuates from a more-or-less circular orbit to a more elliptical one and back again every 405,000 years. It is believed that it is this fluctuating cycle, as well as the play of gravity from other planets, that can significantly affect our Earth climate.[2] However, this recurring elliptical-to-circular orbit really can't explain the three dramatically different orbits in the past as described by Gamarra. It seems that there would have had to be some other mechanism at play for this to happen.

As to what can explain this dramatic, quick shift in Earth's orbit, it seems to me the most likely catalyst to knock Earth out of orbit would have been a significant hit by a large celestial body—like a comet or asteroid or perhaps a moon or planet like the fabled rogue planet Nibiru. There does seem to be evidence for such Earth-moving events. If we look back in Earth's geological record, we see major extinction events that many scientists believe were caused by extraterrestrial bodies hitting the Earth, perhaps bodies large enough to move the planet out of orbit.

Today we know of five major distinct extinction events in Earth's history. A mass extinction event can be defined as a catastrophic global event, such as an asteroid hitting the Earth or widespread climate change that wipes out a large number of species in a relatively short period of geological time. The five major extinction events are:

The Ordovician-Silurian Extinction: 440 million years ago
Devonian Extinction: 365 to 380 million years ago
Permian-Triassic Extinction: 250 million years ago
Triassic-Jurassic Extinction: 210 million years ago
Cretaceous-Tertiary Extinction: 65 Million years ago

There is substantial evidence to believe that four of these extinction events may have been caused by a large asteroid or comet, or a series of them, hitting the Earth. In a 2003 Science.org article, "Devonian Death From Outer Space," Betsy Mason relates the story of geophysicist Brooks Ellwood of Louisiana State University in Baton Rouge, who found evidence of a massive impact in 380-million-year-old rock samples studied in Morocco:

When Ellwood and colleagues returned to Morocco they found several pieces of evidence that are very similar to those found at the K-T boundary (Cretaceaus-Tertiary boundary extinction): high concentrations of nickel, chromium, cobalt, arsenic, and vanadium; a drastic change in the carbon isotope ratio; tiny bits of material called microspherules and microcrysts that formed in the atmosphere from rapidly cooling impact debris; and quartz containing shock fractures that are typically formed by a huge, catastrophic event such as an impact.[4]

At the next major extinction event, the Permian-Triassic, we also find evidence of a violent Earth-shattering event from the heavens. According to Gregory Retallack, a geologist at the University of Oregon, it is believed that a massive asteroid hitting Earth caused this extinction. He bases this hypothesis on the discovery of tiny quartz crystals covered with microscopic fractures found in rocks in Australia and Antarctica that date from the time of the extinction. "You need staggering force, many times greater than a nuclear explosion, to create this shocked quartz," Retallack told *National Geographic*. "Only an impact could deform it [the rock] this way."

The same article describes a 75-mile-wide crater made by an asteroid three miles across, noting that it was not only the impact that caused most of the destruction to the flora and fauna in the Permian-Triassic period but the cascade of other related events including massive volcanism, acid rain, oxygen depletion in the seas, and toxic levels of $CO_2$. Ultimately, some 96 percent of species would die off in this period.[5]

Then we come to the Triassic-Jurassic extinction event, which saw the extinction of 76 percent of all species. In a paper titled "Causes and Consequences of the Triassic-Jurassic Mass Extinction as Seen from the Hartford Basin," Paul E. Olsen, Jessica H. Whiteside, and Philip Huber explain:

We can paint a speculative picture of the Triassic-Jurassic transition. Current data can be explained by the impact of one or more asteroids or comets (e.g. Spray et al., 1998) that terminated biotic diversity, which otherwise was rising through the Late Triassic. As with the K-T scenario, reduced sunlight and lower temperatures plagued continental biotas for months, and the global carbon cycle, as we can see in the abrupt and prolonged negative excursion in carbon isotope composition of marine organic matter.[6]

This assertion is also backed up in the paper, "A Late Triassic Impact Ejecta Layer in Southwestern Britain" by geologists Gordon Walkden, Julian Parker, and Simon Kelley, in which we also find evidence of "shocked" quartz grains that imply a hit by an asteroid:

> Evidence that the impact of an asteroid caused the mass extinctions at the end of the Cretaceous period 65 million years ago made many geologists suspect that a similar impact at the end of the Triassic period caused the mass extinctions then. The Manicouagan crater, one of the largest impact structures on the Earth's surface, was an obvious candidate for the impact site. Previous estimates of its date came with errors that were large enough to overlap with the boundary between the Triassic and Jurassic periods.
>
> The best evidence for an impact at the end of the Triassic was reported by David Bice of Carleton College in Northfield, Minnesota, in late 1990. At the Triassic-Jurassic boundary in Italy, he found "shocked" quartz grains, which are considered evidence of an impact. Bice and others believed that the extinctions occurred rapidly.[7]

So, we have three extinction events that are thought to have been caused by an asteroid or comet before the Cretaceous-Tertiary period, which most scientists are certain was caused by an asteroid. Here UC Davis professor Richard Cowen explains the evidence:

> All over North America, the K-T boundary clay contains glass spherules . . . and just above the clay is a thinner layer that contains iridium along with fragments of shocked quartz. It is only a few millimeters thick, but in total it contains more than a cubic kilometer of shocked quartz in North America alone. The zone of shocked quartz extends west onto the Pacific Ocean floor, but shocked quartz is rare in K-T boundary rocks elsewhere: some very tiny

fragments occur in European sites. All this evidence implies that the K-T impact occurred on or near North America, with the iridium coming from the vaporized asteroid and the shocked quartz coming from the continental rocks it hit.

The K-T impact crater has now been found. It is a roughly egg-shaped geological structure called Chicxulub, deeply buried under the sediments of the Yucatán peninsula of Mexico. . . . The structure is about 180 km across, one of the largest impact structures so far identified with confidence on Earth. A borehole drilled into the Chicxulub structure hit 380 meters (more than 1000 feet) of igneous rock with a strange chemistry. That chemistry could have been generated by melting together a mixture of the sedimentary rocks in the region. The igneous rock under Chicxulub contains high levels of iridium, and its age is 65 Ma, exactly coinciding with the K-T boundary.[8]

It is pretty obvious that we are seeing a pattern here, and a very uncomfortable one to contemplate, with the telltale signs of a massive impact event with the evidence of "shocked" quartz near the impact zones. This stunning revelation that the last four mass extinction events may have been due to an asteroid or a comet directly hitting the Earth is truly eye-opening in its implications—not only for humanity, but all life on this planet.

It makes one pause and wonder at the vulnerability of our fragile blue ball, and ponder what menacing objects are lurking out in space ready to blindside us and possibly wipe us out. We've lived in such a relative time of peace and stability on our planet that it is hard to imagine the complete and utter devastation that happened so many times in the Earth's past, but the evidence is there that our planet has been kicked around violently many times.

With the potential kinetic punch of massive extraterrestrial objects hitting our Earth, is it possible that they could knock Earth out of its orbit? It seems likely.

On November 21, 2021, scientists from NASA attempted to do exactly this, launching the Double Asteroid Redirection Test (DART) mission to nudge the asteroid Dimorphos away from its uncomfortably close orbit to Earth. In a *Washington Post* article, writers Bonnie Berkowitz and Artur Galocha describe how NASA is hoping to change the orbit of an asteroid:

> If all goes well, the spacecraft that NASA plans to launch Tuesday will smash itself to bits against an asteroid.
>
> If all goes absolutely perfectly, that impact will jostle the asteroid into a slightly different orbit, meaning that for the first time, humans will have changed the trajectory of a celestial object.[9]

In fact, the mission was a success, and ten months later, the resulting collision shifted the orbit of Dimorphos by 32 minutes. So the premise that one body hitting another body in space to knock it out of orbit is not one refuted by scientists today. Although an asteroid is much smaller than Earth, it is believed that during the time of a younger Earth there was significantly more debris circulating around in our solar system, with some large enough that an impact with the Earth might have nudged—or whacked—the Earth like a billiard ball from its orbit.

Today we know that there were many minor extinction events, ones like the Younger Dryas period of some 12,800 years ago, a topic the writer Graham Hancock has covered extensively in his recent books. Today scientists have found significant proof that there was an extraterrestrial body, most likely a comet that hit our Earth during this period, causing massive floods and destruction. Many believe that this event was referred to in the Bible and in Sumerian texts as "The Great Flood," and Hancock and others speculate that this one event could have been the one that destroyed Atlantis.

So, acknowledging that it is theoretically possible to have orbital changes from one body hitting another in space, do we have any evidence that this is what happened in the historical record regarding Earth? Alfredo Gamarra brought up two calendars—the Mesoamerican calendar and Sun Gate calendar at Tiwanaku, Bolivia—as representing these distinct orbits. Gamarra also mentioned that the three-stepped chakana and the three rings in the tower of Sacsayhuaman, at Stonehenge in England, and at Borobudur in Indonesia represented these three orbits as well. Let's take a look at these theories to see if there could be something to these ideas.

## THE CALENDARS

According to Alfredo Gamarra, the Mesoamerican (also known as the Aztec or Maya) calendar purportedly shows three Earth orbital cycles of 225, 260, and 365 days. When looking at the iconic calendar you can certainly make out three distinctive rings that may represent these markers of time. There is much written about the 260- and 365-day cycles by historians. The consensus from experts is that the 260-day Tzolkin ritual cycle (sacred round)—called *tonalpohualli* in the Aztec language or *haab* in Maya—was used for understanding individuals' fates.

The 365-day calendar cycle called *xiuhpōhualli* (year count) was used for tracking the passage of time and the seasons of the solar year. The two parts, which make a 52-year cycle, were used to keep chronologies and king lists, mark historical events, date legends, and define the beginning of the world. Unfortunately, I couldn't find much written about the 225-day cycle and what its meaning was. The one account I could find was from Mazatzin Aztekayolokalli, who is an accessor of the ancient culture of Anauak, and an expert on the Mesoamerican calendar. He explains that the 225-day cycle represents the orbit of Venus around the sun—not the Earth—which seems quite plausible as the glyph that marks each day in the 225-day cycle is shown with five dots (see fig. 3.1 p. 51), which is the trajectory of Venus through her journey around the sun over a period of eight years.[10]

This idea that Venus's cycle was central to the calendar seems to have some support. In an article by K. Kris Hirst we read:

> There is growing evidence to believe that the fixed 260-days running from February to October represents the agricultural cycle, keyed to the trajectory of Venus, combined with observations of the Pleiades and eclipse events and potentially appearance and disappearance of Orion.[11]

To back up this claim we can reference a scholarly paper by Susan Milbrath, author of *Ancient Mesoamerica*, in which she writes:

> Research presented here demonstrates that an unusual almanac in the Madrid Codex (pages 12–18) integrates observations of the Venus cycle with eclipse events in the context of the agricultural year. Imagery in the 260-day almanac represents eclipse glyphs associated with Tzolkin dates that coordinate with eclipses visible in Yucatan during the fifteenth century, indicating the almanac dates to the Late Postclassic. The almanac also depicts seasonal events in the context of a repeating pattern of paired solar eclipses associated with observations of Venus as the evening star. Quetzalcoatl-Kukulcan's counterpart in the Madrid almanac is the Chicchan serpent, who plays the role of Venus in a sequence showing a fertile aspect of the planet linked with the 260-day agricultural cycle and the Pleiades. Clearly, Venus positions and eclipse events were closely watched in relation to the planting cycle, reflecting a form of "agro-astronomy" that we are only now beginning to understand.[12]

It would seem that the inner 225-day Venus calendar is very likely to correspond to the 260-day agricultural calendar, which backs up Mazatzin Aztekayolokalli's claim that the 225-day cycle is the orbit of Venus around the sun. Unfortunately, if this is correct this would seem

Fig. 3.1. The Mesoamerican calendar. According to Mazatzin Aztekayolokalli, Indigenous wisdom keeper, the 225-day Venus orbit cycle is shown in increments of five dots (outlined in dark grey). Photo credit Gary Todd.

to discount Gamarra's claim that the calendar represents the three different Earth orbits.

Gamarra also mentions the Tiwanaku Sun Gate calendar as showing these three orbits. He seems to have some support—at least in the notion that the Earth had at one time a different orbit—via the work of Professor Hans Schindler-Bellamy. Schindler-Bellamy co-wrote *The Calendar of Tiahuanaco* with Peter Allen. In this book Schindler-Bellamy and Allen not only claim that the Sun Gate is a calendar from a civilization more than twelve-thousand years ago, but that this calendar differs from the present because at that time Earth had a different solar orbit and axial tilt, and a different moon. The belief that the Earth had a different moon was probably due to the fact that Hans Schindler-Bellamy was an authority on the writer and researcher Hanns Hobiger, who originally promoted such a theory.

There is also Arthur Posnansky, the so-called Father of Bolivian archaeology, as well as cartographer James Allen, and Dominican priest Jose Domingo Duquesne, who have all done extensive examinations of the calendar and seem to be in agreement that this calendar marked solar cycles (Posnansky) and sun and moon cycles (Allen and Duquesne) based on a very complex Muisca-Acrotom system. Here is a brief summation of this strange system by Duquesne, who claimed to have been given this information from the Amyara people at the time:

> Twenty moons, then, made the year. When these were finished, they counted another twenty, and thus successively, continuing in a continuous circle until concluding twenty times twenty. The inclusion of one moon, which it is necessary to make after the thirty-sixth, so that the lunar year corresponded to the solar year, and thus they conserved the regularity of the seasons, which they did with consummate ease.

According to Allen:

> At Tiwanaku we found how the solar year was divided into 20 months of 18 days and also interlocked with the Inca calendar of 12 sidereal lunar months of 27.32 days (making 328 days) so that 3 x solar years also equaled 40 sidereal lunar months, and the two calendars came together every 18 solar years, which equaled 20 Inca years when the cycle started all over again (also known as the Saros Cycle).*[13]

Although many researchers argue that the Tiwanaku Sun Gate is a calendar, many archaeologists have disputed this, as they tried to make

---

*If you wish to dive in deep into this subject matter, I refer you to the article "The Gate of the Sun Calendar from Ancient Tiwanacu"[14] by Kenneth MacLean, who encapsulated the work of the above-cited individuals.

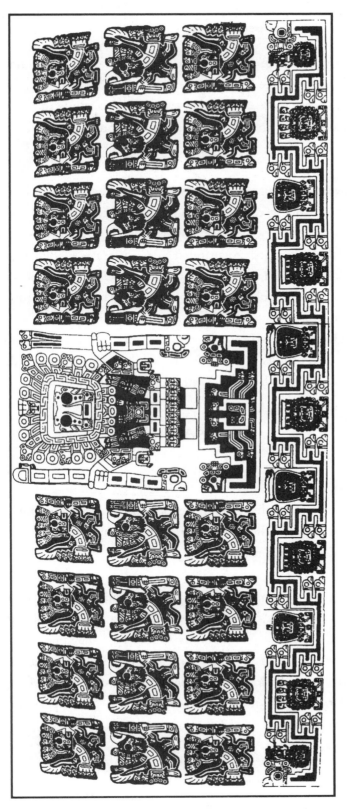

Fig. 3.2. Drawing of the Gate of the Sun calendar at Tiwanaku with eleven chasqui heads on the bottom, representing the 11 pillars at Kalasasaya "which in turn divide the solar year into 20 months of 18 days, and the 40 condor heads represent the 40 sidereal months which mesh with the solar calendar every three years."[15]

sense of this calendar in terms of our present solar year, and gave up when they couldn't make it work. They later declared that it was nothing but an intricate piece of art. However, many continue to insist the sculpture is a calendar, though one of a special kind, designed for a special purpose, and, of course, for a special time—a time with a different solar year.

The Tiwanaku calendar, if that is what it really is, is probably one of the most confusing calendars I have ever encountered. I confess that I am not ready to go into extensive study of it; however, I did want to highlight it as it is mentioned by Gamarra as evidence of the Three Worlds—albeit, I am not exactly sure how. It may demonstrate a shorter (and closer orbit) around the sun, as Schindler-Bellamy and Allen suggest.

Although the calendar is not entirely convincing for the Three World orbital hypothesis, it does seem to hold some promise of a different orbital cycle from which the Earth might have transitioned.

## THE CHAKANA AND SITES WITH THREE CIRCLES

The chakana, or Andean cross and three-stepped symbol, and the sites of Sacsayhuaman, Stonehenge, and Borobudur, were all mentioned by Gamarra as evidence of the Three World cosmogony. In a paper written by Jan Peter de Jong, we read:

> According to Alfredo, the 3-sided double stepped motif, a symbol found all over in the Inca culture, is also a reflection of this concept of 3 different periods/orbits/worlds. And the same would be the case with a concept of 3 circles used in vestiges all over the World, like the 3 circles of Stonehenge, the 3 circles on top of the Borobudur, and the 3 circles of the Moyuc Marka, at the upper part of Sacsayhuaman.[16]

Let's first look at the chakana symbol to see if we can find any clues that this symbol was used to represent three orbits.

Like Jan Peter says, the chakana symbol was used widely by the Inca, but this wasn't just confined to the Inca culture. We can see that this symbol was used widely in the Chavín, Wari, and Tiwanaku cultures as well, cultures that significantly pre-date the Incas. Usually, the symbol is represented as a three-stepped ascending and descending stairway on two sides, but sometimes it is reflected in four dimensions, which represent the four cardinal points marking the solstices, equinoxes, and the four provinces of the Incan empire (Tawantinsuyu): Chinchaysuyo, Kollasuyo, Antisuyo, and Contisuyo.[17] Frequently, it is worn as a talisman and pendant in the two-dimensional configuration. The half chakana is seen at many significant sacred sites in Peru, like those at the ruins of Pisac and at Machu Picchu.

However, like with the Mayan and Tiwanaku calendars, it isn't exactly clear if this symbol represents three distinct orbital cycles of the Earth or represents the three worlds in Andean cosmology. For clarity's sake, the three worlds in Andean cosmology have different connotations to the definitions that Gamarra uses to classify the geological time periods and styles of architecture. For instance, in Andean cosmology the three worlds reflect the concepts of a higher, spiritual world, also called Hanan Pacha and is represented by the condor, a middle world that describes our present-day world called *Kay Pacha*, represented by a puma, and a lower world composed of nature spirits and elementals referred to as *Uku Pacha*, represented by the snake. This Andean cosmology represents the layers of our spiritual and physical realities and is by far the most common interpretation of the chakana symbol's meaning. I have heard that there is an even more esoteric meaning to the chakana than the three worlds as expressed in Andean cosmology, but I don't know what that is, and it seems to be a well-guarded secret by those who really do know. I wonder if the more esoteric meaning is related to the Gamarra's Three Orbits and Three Worlds theories; however, this is pure speculation.

It has been observed that the half chakana at Machu Picchu casts a shadow on the June solstice (see fig. 3.4), which purportedly represents the dark, spiritual realm of existence in the dual nature of reality.

There are also issues regarding Gamarra's interpretation with the examples of Stonehenge, Borobudur, and Moyuc Marka, as there is nothing in the historical record that would indicate that the three circular rings at these sites represent three orbits. As far as I can find, the beautiful Javanese temple of Borobudur represents the sacred mountain of Mount Meru, and it is designed for the pilgrim to meditate on as he circumambulates on his ascent up this symbolic mountain. The three circles seem to represent the top layers of the superior, nonmaterial realm of existence. According to a paper by John M. Lundquist, in which he explores the top terraces of the temple:

> . . . the mountain/temple in a circumambulating fashion (pradaksina), takes the initiate through an elaborate process of learning the sacred doctrines by means of the reliefs carved into the square galleries of the first four levels . . . There are four hundred thirty-two Buddhas arranged along the four sides of the lower balustrades, giving the appearance, from a distance, of Siddhas meditating deep within caves on the sides of the sacred mountain. As the initiate would reach the platform on which the elliptical and circular levels were raised, he would have reached the summit of [Mount] Meru, having left the world of appearances of the lower, gallery level.[18]

The author's paper explains in detail the symbolic meaning of the upper terraces of the monument. However, I can find nothing to indicate the three circles on the top are representative of three orbits. This is also the case with Stonehenge. The only reference I can find to orbits being symbolically represented in its construction are found on online forums, and those mainly cover the idea that the circles represent orbits of the inner planets in our solar system. I can find nothing scholarly, or

Fig. 3.3. The Chakana stone at
Machu Picchu (bottom right).

Fig. 3.4. Chakana at Machu Picchu.
McKay Savage.

for that matter speculative, about three Earth orbits represented by the circular structures.

One thing that's clear is that Stonehenge is definitely acknowledged by scholars as a solar calendar and that the massive rocks, equally spaced out, act as a clock to mark time and the equinoxes and solstices.

As far as the tower foundation platform of Moyuc Marka in Sacsayhuaman, though it does show three concentric circles—which, theoretically, could describe these three orbits—it seems that Gamarra is the only one proposing they are so, so it is hard to ascribe meaning to this monument.

■ ■ ■

In conclusion, though there does seem to be some hypothetical support for Gamarra's Three Earth Orbits theory—especially if we could establish that the Earth had been knocked out of orbit due to massive extraterrestrial objects hitting it—this hypothesis hasn't been seriously examined by mainstream geologists, and I have my doubts it ever will be. Regarding any evidence for these three different orbits found in historical records and at archaeological sites, Alfredo Gamarra claimed to have received many of his insights about these three worlds in his dreams, and they may very well be valid. Unfortunately, there is just not enough supporting evidence to definitively prove the chakana symbol, temples, and structures with three circles, as well the Mesoamerican and Tiwanaku calendars, represent these different orbits.

However, the lack of supporting evidence in the historical and archaeological records for these three orbits is not enough for me to abandon Gamarra's more mainstream theories. His other theories hold up to scrutiny very well. For instance, we can see in the archaeological record three distinct cultures represented by the evidence of three distinct building styles and techniques, as well as overbuilding, with the oldest culture on the bottom and later cultures on top. We can also see that Hanan Pacha and Uran Pacha forms have evidence of vitrification, which is a process of using extremely high heat to change the chemistry of rock, and today can be proven by fluorescence chemical analysis. Also, we have evidence that Hanan Pacha and Uran Pacha rocks were at one time soft enough to mold. Today, these ideas are being backed up with mainstream science.[19]

At one time, all of these theories were heresy to mainstream archaeology, and still are in some circles today, but with new evidence from modern forensic tools and analysis, we seem to be entering into a new golden age of archaeology, an era that can shine light on the physical evidence Gamarra pointed out a long time ago. If anything, Alfredo Gamarra had a keen eye for observation of physical anomalies that archaeologists at the time couldn't see—or accept. Gamarra, by being outside the constraints and conventions of academia, has opened up the dialogue regarding what our ancestors were capable of in the past, and as a consequence, helped to change the way we see history.

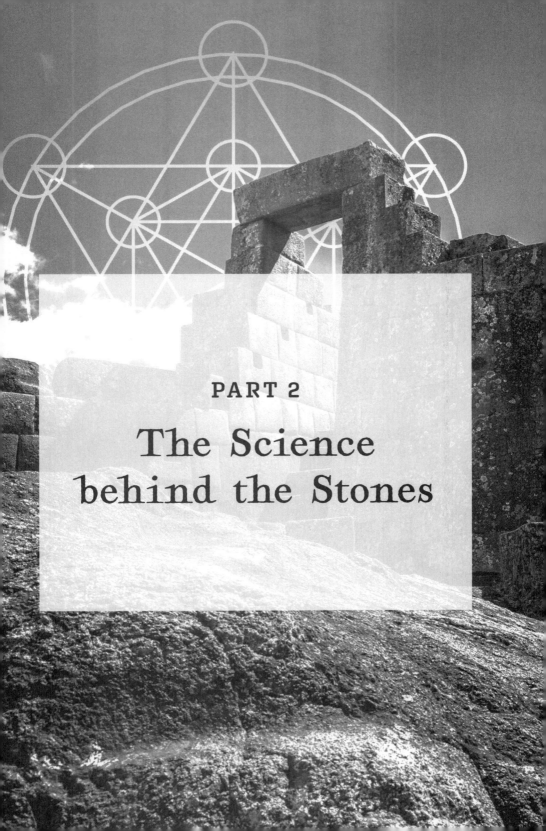

PART 2

# The Science
# behind the Stones

# 4

# Feeling High?
# Wakas and
# Altered States

*At our most elemental, we are not a chemical reaction, but an energetic charge.*

LYNNE McTAGGART, *THE FIELD*

Why do so many find the temples and megalithic sites around the world so fascinating? Millions travel every year to see Egyptian, Greek, Middle Eastern, Indian, Chinese, and Central and South American pyramids and temple complexes. I think that part of the appeal is to see and experience the greatness of these ancient monuments, and wonder at the mysterious people who built them. But besides the awe and wonder that these sites inspire, some people recognize them as places designed to facilitate altered states of consciousness.

Sacred sites researcher and best-selling author Freddy Silva has spent many years of his life exploring how these temples and megalithic sites are strategically put in certain areas to enhance the telluric currents and electromagnetic fields already present in the environment. He describes the effects that visitors to these sites can feel:

> It doesn't take much to stimulate the human body's electro-magnetic circuitry, in fact a small change in the local environment is enough to create a change in awareness.
>
> People who visit ancient temples and megalithic sites often describe such a sensation. The standard explanation is that such feelings are nothing more than a "wow" factor: the result of visual stimuli from the overwhelming impression generated by megalithic constructions such as stone circles, ancient temples and pyramids.
>
> But the cumulative evidence proves otherwise: that megaliths and other ancient sacred places are actually attracting, storing, even generating their own energy field, creating the kind of environment where one can enter an altered state of consciousness.[1]

I can personally attest to the truth in this, as I have found myself in various forms of altered states when visiting certain sites around Peru. One of the most profound experiences that I had was at a relatively unknown waka near the Moon Temple complex in Sacsayhuaman. I don't know its official name, as it remains unmarked, and because of its diminutive stature most visitors just walk right past it on the way to the well-known Temple de la Luna. However, if you go into the small cave under the beehive-shaped mound, and if you are sensitive enough, you can feel the unique energy of the place. The few times I have been there, I have always walked out with shaky legs and feeling quite light-headed after a short meditation, and this unmistakably intense energy is not lost on other spiritual seekers and shamans, who often leave copious amounts of coca leaves as offerings to Pacha Mama and the *apus* (mountain spirits) in the cave alcove.

A similar experience happened to me at Ñaupa Waka (sometimes called Ñaupa Iglesia), a portal site near the small town of Pachar in the Sacred Valley. After a coca offering, I put my forehead on the enigmatic blue-gray throne rock and either I, or the rock, started vibrating so much that I thought I was experiencing an earthquake. When I asked my friends behind me if they thought we had had an earthquake they all said that they had felt nothing.

And in 2021, I visited the White Rock (Yurac Rumi) in the archaeology complex of Ñusta Hispana in Vilcabamba with my friend, Francisco. Even though I didn't get an immediate tingly feeling while at the site, later at night, back in my hotel room, I had a powerful white flash strike me in my pineal gland—one so bright and powerful I shot out of bed in shock. Though I cannot say for sure if it was my visit to the White Rock that precipitated the coursing bolt of electricity running through me, I felt in my heart that that was the cause of the flash.

Because of these powerful experiences at various sacred sites, I've often thought that there is something about how and where these sites are built that channels energy and focuses it. I have read that a lot of these monolithic and megalithic sites are constructed with rock containing high quartz content, and some of them, like the triple-throne rock at Ñaupa Waka, are magnetic, and can channel and focus the strength of electromagnetic currents.[2] Here Silva mentions how certain rocks can attract this energy:

> The effect of sacred sites behaving like concentrators of electromagnetic energy is enhanced by the choice of stone. Often moved across enormous distances, the stone used in megalithic sites contains substantial amounts of magnetite. The combination makes temples behave like weak, albeit huge, magnets.[3]

In a study to investigate the electromagnetic properties of 80,000 menhirs (giant standing stones) at the Carnac region of France, electrical engineer Pierre Mereaux, who was originally a skeptic of any electromagnetic properties being generated by the stones, concluded that there was indeed proof that the stones were attracting and concentrat-

Fig. 4.1. Precision stone masonry to the side and below
Yurac Rumi (White Rock). See also color plate 9.

ing electromagnetic forces because of their high quartz composition and
location:

> The dolmen (menhir) behaves as a coil or solenoid, in which cur-
> rents are induced, provoked by the variations, weaker or stronger,
> of the surrounding magnetic field. But these phenomena are not
> produced with any intensity unless the dolmen is constructed with
> crystalline rocks rich in quartz, such as granite.
>
> Because of the very high quartz content in the stones, they are par-
> ticularly piezoelectric, which is to say they generate electricity when

compressed or subjected to vibrations. Mereux believes that because the megaliths of Carnac are positioned upon thirty-one fracture zones of the most active earthquake area in France, they are in a constant state of vibration, making the stones electromagnetically active.[4]

Pierre Mereaux's study showed how the menhirs amplify and release telluric energy throughout the day, with the strongest readings occurring at dawn (this is something I heard from a shaman at Ñaupa Waka as well), and that the readings also show a regular pulsation of energy at intervals at the base of the stone. These currents are positively and negatively charged, and were recorded up to thirty-six feet from these monoliths. Mereaux also recorded extreme pulsations that recycle approximately every seventy minutes, showing that the menhirs charge and discharge regularly.

Just how these electromagnetic fluctuations and currents affect the human body seems to be well known to the ancients who built these structures, and today some modern scientists are beginning to catch up with how geophysical forces can have significant impacts on one's well-being.

In a scientific paper titled, "The Effects of Geophysical Anomalies on Biology," the authors write:

> Architecture, as currently practiced, does not take into account the possible effect of the ground from the point of view of geophysical anomalies created by various geological features.
>
> Earth radiation anomalies are related to various phenomena, such as the piezoelectricity, radioactivity, geochemical gasses, seismic faults, gravity anomalies, electromagnetic emission, electro-kinetic phenomena of subterranean water flow, spinning electric fields, ion flow, conductivity discontinuities, non-dipolar magnetic fields, geoplasma, and geoneutrons. Specific geological materials can also alter and/or augment these phenomena.[5]

The paper specifically looks at how these combined factors can interact with the biology of humans, plants, and animals, and one of the areas that caught my attention in the paper was the mention of a hydro-geophysical phenomenon, which the paper describes as "a low-intensity electric current and hence the magnetic field associated with it, created by the friction between groundwater and porous limestone rocks as the water molecules attempt to pass though the rock's micro tunnels within its matrix."

As anyone who has spent a large amount of time investigating Hanan Pacha sites in Peru will notice, almost all of them are built of limestone and are almost always built on top of, or near, running water sources. Why is this significant? As the paper mentions, "The presence of limestone has a strong interaction with water flow, as its geological interstructure is perfect for the production of natural electricity by hydro-geophysical means . . . . Electrons are removed from the rainwater as it passes through the porosity of the rock and are attached to it, in a process called adsorption."[6]

We can see at the limestone monoliths at Sacsayhuaman, and in other watery areas like Quillabamba, Vilcabamba, and Chinchero, that there is significant water seepage and erosion of the limestone wakas, with the telltale greenish black mold features forming where the water is breaking down the limestone. Frequently I have noticed that this blackened moldy area is where many spiritual visitors leave coca leaves as offerings.

One psychic told me that a darkened moldy area to the left of the Ñaupa Waka's cave entrance was a portal, which I found interesting as it was directly opposite the granite alcove that most people associate with the Ñaupa portal. Sure enough, when I looked closely, I noticed that others detected this area as a special location, evidenced by abundance of coca leaves and other offerings at the base of the rock. Can both the black moldy areas in the limestone and the granite portal at Ñaupa help to facilitate inter-dimensional communication and altered states? And what about the bluestone with the triple-throne that sits between these two areas? How were they used in conjunction with the portal(s)?

Fig. 4.2. Mold from water seepage on a Chinchero waka.

Fig. 4.3. The bluestone throne area of Ñaupa Waka.

On one of my many trips to this site I overheard an Indigenous guide explain to a group that the left-side seat represents the feminine principle and the right-side seat the masculine, which is consistent with the Andean duality-based spiritual tradition. Was the middle area throne designed for an initiate to transcend his dual nature and become what in the Western traditions is called Great Hermaphrodite, a reconciliation of spirit and matter, a being of both male and female qualities? And did the portals to the left and right of the thrones generate an electromagnetic current to help the spiritual seeker have an out-of-body experience or the needed shift in consciousness to know her higher self? It is plausible to me. The shift of consciousness that I have experienced there, minus plant medicines and ceremony, was very strong. If one is under the influence of San Pedro (or *huachuma* as it commonly referred to here), a cactus that grows on the mountain where Ñaupa resides, and has gone into a trance (maybe with the help of an Andean *paco*), I can certainly see how this site could facilitate shamanic journeys and altered states.

There is also a cave in the back of the bluestone throne and portals, and it is filled in with rubble—probably by the authorities to discourage anyone from going inside. But if you climb over the ledge above the cave, you will find a large hole that goes straight down into a cavern connecting to the cave below. Examining this layout at its orientation, it seems like an ideal place for an initiation, which will be explored in chapter five.

## FREE ENERGY THROUGH THE ELEMENTS

I found this insightful comment by the late Egyptian archaeologist and wisdom-keeper Abd'el Hakim Awyan who said (in very broken English) in part two of the documentary series *The Pyramid Code:*

And it [here he is referring to explosive energy] is not the only energy on our planet. There are plenty: the rivers flow by energy;

tsunami is energy; frequencies are energy. If we have the electricity now, it is based on explosion energy. Now the sound energy based on the technology, it is different from the explosion energy—it is known as implosion energy. Our energy all over the planet today is based on explosion energy—that's why petrol is expensive (haha!). Implosion energy is very simple—all that you need is the beam of the Sun on running water; not just running in a straight line but in a zigzag, that is why you will find all the tunnels are in a zigzag form for such a purpose.[7]

I was very surprised and excited to have found this comment by Awyan, as it seemed to confirm a theory that I had been entertaining regarding the walls of Sacsayhuaman, and that was that the zigzag walls were not just for defensive purposes, as most historians believe, but may have been used to generate energy. This idea came to me one day after I looked down from one of the higher-walled platforms and noticed that there seemed to be water channels cut between the zigzag walls. At the time I thought that this didn't make sense as the walls are supposed to be military fortifications. Why would you build water channels through them if that were the case? The thought came to me: "Wouldn't it make more sense that the water running between the stone walls were somehow getting charged and somehow acting as a power generator?"

This thought came to me after reading an archaeo-architecture paper about how there once were extensive waterworks in and around the Muyuc Marca area at Sacsayhuaman. This area once had three towers that were later torn down during the time of the Spanish conquest to build the city of Cusco. Archaeologists discovered that these towers had water hydraulic systems built into them, and it was believed that there was a natural spring below the biggest tower, Muyuc Marca.[7] With the zigzag walls surrounding these towers, could these towers have been used to broadcast a tone or frequency to the population at the time? Maybe to be used for the health and well-being of the population, or to help crops grow?

Fig. 4.4. Sacsayhuaman from above.
Courtesy of Jan Peter de Jong.

I also discovered that there is a complex network of zigzag tunnels under the Akapana Pyramid in the Tiwanaku complex. Tiwanaku was the site thought to be the home to the Andean savior God Viracocha Kon Tiki so this is significant as Virachocha's lore in the Andes is great. Was this pyramid, which was at one time in the past very near the banks of Lake Titicaca, some kind of power generator? If so, what for?

It turns out there is some solid evidence that some megalithic sites were designed to improve crop yields. The late author, scientist, and businessman John Burke created a company based on his extensive research into crops near megalith sites.

Burke and his partner, Kaj Halberg, describe how seeds that were placed at megalithic sites and mounds were positively stressed by the ambient electromagnetic currents, which resulted in higher propagation rates, quicker maturity, and improved crop yields.

They speculated that perhaps many of the sites that we call "sacred sites" are only considered so because today's modern archaeologists and historians don't know what their original purpose was, and, as a consequence, they are thought to be ceremonial. In their excellent, but now out-of-print book *Seed of Knowledge, Stone of Plenty*, Burke and Halberg explain that many of these sites were utilitarian:

> However, the "ceremonial site" label is simply an interpretation that has, over time, become enshrined as fact. Among academics working in the field, no one could think of any practical use for a Stonehenge or a pyramid. So, if they were devoid of practical purpose, they must have been used only for ceremony. This reasoning has become so ingrained in our view of prehistory that these structures are often referred to as "sacred sites."
>
> We need to remember that we view these sites through the tinted glasses of our own culture, which divorces the spiritual from the practical.[8]

As to how the process of electromagnetism in the Earth works, the authors explain that the strongest fields are produced when two disparate fields are next to one another:

> When dawn brings a change in magnetic field strength, it actually generates weak DC currents in the ground. Like all electric currents, these telluric currents travel better in some media than others. Ground with lots of metal or water within it conducts these natural, daily currents particularly well. Drier or less metallic ground conducts it less well.
>
> When these two types of land intersect, we have what geologists call a conductivity discontinuity, and interesting things happen there. The ground current hitting this boundary has a tendency to either reinforce or weaken those daily magnetic fluctuations—sometimes by several hundred percent. This change in magnetic field strength in turn generates more electric current. So conductivity discontinuities are "happening places." Their magnetic fluctuations and ground currents are much higher than in surrounding areas.[9]

Burke and Halberg, based on their own experiments, postulate that many of these monuments do in fact produce physical effects, which are still felt today. Plus, they found that many mounds, pyramids, and hedges were built on ground where certain natural electromagnetic energies are concentrated, and designed in such a way as to further concentrate these energies for the end result of producing more food.

On a recent trip to Lake Titicaca I was introduced to the raised agricultural beds called *waru-waru* that look very similar to the type of crop circles that we see in England. My guide, Beto, who grew up in the area, told me that the crops near this area grow healthier and faster than other places in the Altiplano without such features. Scientists who have studied these sites say that the canals that run between the raised beds are solar heat traps used to keep crops alive during the often-freezing nights. They also say that these beds create artificial ecosystems to attract birds and fish that supplement the diet of the locals. It was also believed that these canals could reduce soil erosion and flooding.[10] It is unclear as to whether any research has been done to validate if these sites produced an electromagnetic field, but it certainly seems possible knowing how water, sun, and the earth interact with one another.

It also seems like the archaeological site of Moray in the high Andes could be one such place for harnessing earth energies to generate higher crop yields. Moray is one of the most visited tourist destinations in Peru, known for its picturesque vistas. It is believed that

Fig. 4.5. Lake Titicaca waru-waru or crop circle.

Moray functioned as a center for agricultural experimentation, and that each level in its terracing offered a different climatic environment, allowing for different plants to be grown.[11] Could the flowing lines and circles incorporated in the site have been used to enhance the growth of crops as well by concentrating telluric currents?

Fig. 4.6. Moray agricultural site.
See also color plate 10.

Although the authors of *Seed of Knowledge* do think that many megaliths and mounds were used for food production, they also acknowledge that sacred sites were used to generate altered states of consciousness. They mention that within the anthropological community it is largely accepted that the rock art was likely created by shamans in a trance state, depicting their own hallucinations on the rock. Additionally, they mention that the geological structures around the Petroglyph National Monument are located on powerful magnetic fields created by powerful electrical ground currents, and that the shamans specifically sought out these locations for their mind altering properties.

Burke relates his own altered state experience when visiting the 7,242 foot Black Elk Peak, a sacred place to the Black Hills tribes in North Dakota: After measuring electrical ground currents some 200 feet below the summit with his assistant, Burke took a needed rest and put his head on the cliff face. After closing his eyes he writes "dizziness and disorientation were the immediate results." He soon realized that when he took his head off the rock, the effect stopped, but would start again if he put his head back on the rock. Later, he noticed that there was a vertical vein of quartz running through the rock and when he tested it with his meter he saw that a strong electrical charge was coming from it, creating charged air.

This question of altered states at sacred sites will certainly be relevant in the next section where we will explore if some of these wakas were used as initiation sites and to facilitate communication with other worlds.

# 5

# Chambers
# for Initiation

*Far from being dead and forgotten, ancient temples are as alive as the day they were built, and anyone who has visited Stonehenge or Saqqara, not as a tourist but as a pilgrim, understands this.*

FREDDY SILVA, *THE DIVINE BLUEPRINT*

It is the contention of ancient mystery researcher and author Freddy Silva that certain sacred sites are used for initiations, and he points to two sites in particular at Sacsayhuaman—Little Chinkana and Q'enko—as fitting the physical requirements for initiation rituals.

Silva says that both sites are oriented in an east–west configuration, and they align with Venus rising to the east on the spring equinox. Silva said these initiatory rites were practiced all over the world in ancient times, and consisted of the candidate(s) entering a cave on the west side at sunset—which represents the underworld, as well as the candidates' neophyte status. After spending a certain amount of time in this underworld—according to some, three days—if the candidates don't go crazy, or worse, die, they emerge from the chamber or cave to greet Venus as she rises in the east. If the journey went well, the person is called "reborn."

I've been to both of these sites many times, and I tend to agree with Silva that they are initiation sites. One can see at Little Chinkana a cave complex opposite the ticket booth, and a very distinctive chamber to the west where I believe the candidates spent their time dwelling in the underworld. After being roused from their (possibly) drug-induced slumber, where they journeyed to other dimensions, they made their way through the winding, pitch-black, and very claustrophobic cave to emerge, greeting Venus, and then the rising sun, purportedly newly reborn.

At Q'enko, the Ministry of Culture, it would seem, has people going into the cave complex the wrong way—from east to west. But I don't think their concerns relate to initiation rites for tourists, nor do I think they even have any sense that the cave was originally intended for that purpose.

The official narrative in regard to the cave complex at Q'enko is that it was used to mummify the Inca nobility, and that certainly may be the case, as many ancient sites were used by later cultures for their own purposes. However, there are some clear indications that Silva may be right about Q'enko being an initiation chamber. For example, in the west part of the cave there is a stairway heading down into a beehive-shaped cave entrance (see fig. 5.1 p. 78), which would take one to the chamber underneath the rock—a place indicating the underworld. There you can see a number of polished platforms that can hold full-sized bodies, and, near the iconic "altar" platform (fig. 5.3 p. 79), there are three steps which could symbolically indicate the three worlds (fig. 5.4 p. 79) that the candidate would have to negotiate to become reborn.

After the candidates' required time navigating in other worlds, they would emerge from the chamber and walk up the stairs, indicating their emergence out of the underworld, to face Venus on the equinox. This follows the inclination line of the perfectly carved rock to the left. Can this be a coincidence?

Fig. 5.1 & Fig. 5.2. Entrance into Q'enko chamber looking
down and up.

After considering the idea that some sites were used as initiation
chambers, I also thought that Ñaupa Waka might be one, as it too is
oriented in an east–west trajectory, especially when looking out from
the cave entrance. There is also an inverted $V$ shape above the entrance
to the cave, which has an angle of fifty-two degrees on one side and sixty
degrees on the other. Silva points out in an article—"Naupa Iglesia: An
Egyptian Portal in the Andes?"—that "[t]here is only one other place on
earth where these two numbers appear side by side: the slope angles of
the two major pyramids at Giza."

Fig. 5.3. The altar of the Q'enko chamber.

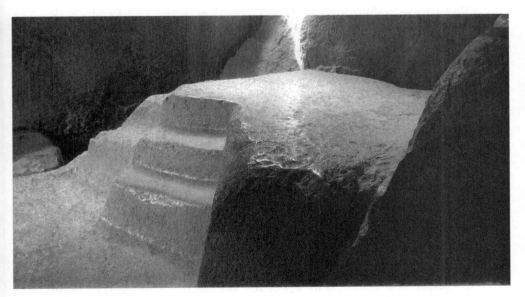

Fig. 5.4. Three-step rock to the left of the Q'enko altar.

We also learn from the same article that the main portal or "spirit" door holds some rather significant ratios that conform to musical notations. "The length to height ratio is 3:1, making a perfect fifth in the second octave; the ratio of the alcove is 5:6, a minor third," and once again we see some numbers that encode some significant ratios about the planet:

> The 5:6 ratio is both unusual and filled with specialist information. It perfectly describes the movement of the Earth, whose pole completes one full rotation of its axis every 25,920 years, while the plane of the equator tilts four degrees every 21,000 years—a ratio of 5:6. This accurate calculation of the motion of the planet is also encoded in another unusual temple, the Bent Pyramid of Egypt, whose slope angles encode the same ratio. [1]

Might all these musical keys and esoteric numbers be used by a priest using sound and chant to help an initiate, who may be under the influence of some kind of hallucinogen, reach another dimension? Also, could sacred sound and geomagnetic lines be used to call other beings from another dimension to the portal area? I feel it could. I have been there many times and have encountered many pacos (shamans) and spiritual seekers doing ceremonies there. To me it has a very magical feel to it and I always pay homage to the spirits of the place with coca leaves and flowers.

## MAPPING THE CONSTELLATIONS

According to Edwin Salazar Garcés, author of *Astronomia Inka*, and the scientific director of Planetarium Cusco, there are other encoded numbers at the site. Garcés is an expert on the relationship between architecture and astronomy. He says that the axes of the bluestone thrones, projected at certain stars and constellations marked certain significant days in the Andean calendar.

Fig. 5.5. The "spirit door" at Ñaupa Waka.

For instance, around the time of 1500 CE an axis from the first chamber seat (to the left) has an azimuth of 149 degrees and points to the exit of the Southern Cross (from the line site of a mountain peak marker on the opposite side of Ñaupa Waka) on April 26. This was the day of the sun's nadir (the lowest point on the horizon) and marked the beginning of the big harvest in the month of May.

Carcés writes that on chamber two there is an axis with an azimuth of 137 degrees that points to the center of the star Sargas (a bright star in the tail section of the Scorpion Constellation) on June 21. This day indicates the time when the sun is at its zenith during the winter solstice in the Southern Hemisphere and marks the Inca's holiest day, Inti Raymi.

And on chamber three an axis with an aximuth of 102–103 degrees points to the exit of star Sirius (also known as Wilkawara in Quechua) and marks the sowing season around August 18 in the year 1500 CE.

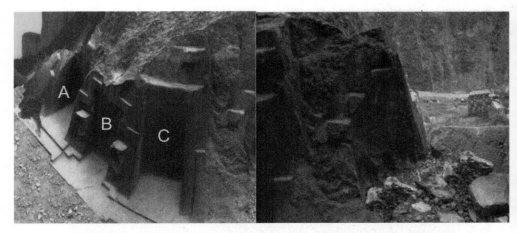

Fig. 5.6. Ñaupa Waka bluestones axes point to key constellations.

This same alignment also marks the Summer Solstice time of Qhapaq Raymi on December 23.

Does this indicate that the triple throne (fig. 5.6) was put there and used by the Incas sometime in the 1500s? Maybe, or perhaps this bluestone could be much older, as we do know that the Earth has an axial precession relative to the fixed stars that recurs approximately every 26,000 years. Is it possible that people long before the Inca, and for the same purpose (or to mark other significant events), could have used those axes marks?

Whatever the true story, it seems from all indications that Ñaupa Waka was not only used as an observatory to mark celestial events, but also an initiation site, since there is no reason to have a portal there if it were only an observatory. According to Freddy Silva, "Temples of a similar nature in other parts of the world typically require a difficult access, followed by a sensory deprived environment which generates conditions for the candidate to access other levels of reality."[3] Ñaupa certainly fits that description. Not only must the climber ascend up a very steep and challenging incline, but the incline itself, from start to finish, represents the three worlds, with a cave on the bottom representing the underworld, another shrine a bit more than halfway up representing the middle world, and on the top, the portal, cave, and throne area representing the spiritual world. The cave on top is possibly where the candidate would go (maybe lowered in through the top chamber above the cave) as the sensory deprivation part of the ritual. At a certain time the candidate would come out to greet the sun.

■ ■ ■

I have mixed feelings about writing about Ñaupa Waka. It is only a small site and I hope it does not become too popular or a part of the tourist circuit. I would hate to see the wrappers and plastic bottles that more unconscious travelers frequently leave behind littered around the site, or lines of people waiting for their chance to take selfies at the portal. Right now pacos and spiritual groups still mainly use it, and I hope it stays that way. It truly is a sacred place and I hope it will be seen and appreciated as one.

# 6

# Sacred Sites
# and Sound Healing

*The ancients understood that a simple sound could reorganize the body's structure. Sounds that are harmonious, activate the body and create healing.*

BARBARA MARCINIAK, *EARTH: PLEIADIAN KEYS TO THE LIVING LIBRARY*

In chapter four we explored how megalithic sites could affect one's physical being and consciousness via the electromagnetic properties of the sites themselves combined with the Earth's geophysical properties. In chapter five we looked at their possible use for initiation. In this chapter we will explore how sound and chant may have been a factor in their design as well.

When I lived in Hawaii I was blessed to meet Dorian Carter, now in her eighties, who was a professional musician and teacher for most of her life. She told me that one day when she was meditating in Sedona she received a message from the Pleiades about how to heal through sound. I was very surprised by this, as this woman did not strike me as New Age-y, but as someone very down to Earth.

**Plate 1.** The Temple of the Condor at Machu Picchu.

**Plate 2.** Uran Pacha overbuilding on Hanan Pacha monolith, Pisac, Peru.

**Plate 3.** The author in front of a
giant polygonal stone at the Sacsayhuaman citadel, Peru.

**Plate 4.** "The Foundation Stone"
by Carl Haag.

**Plate 5.** Hanan Pacha forms at Little Q'enko, Sacsayhuaman.

**Plate 6.** Inca construction in the northern part of Sacsayhuaman Park.

**Plate 7.** Uran Pacha polygonal stones surround Colina Suchuna, a Hanan Pacha site.

Plate 8. Ancient quarry or ancient waka? Banbaura, Japan.

**Plate 9.** Precision stone masonry to the side and below
Yurac Rumi (White Rock) in Vilcabamba, Peru.

Plate 10. Moray agricultural site.

**Plate 11.** Inner structure of a chullpa shows a
beehive chamber. Sillustani, Peru.

**Plate 12.** Pumapunku stonework, Bolivia.

Plate 13. A detail of
the Saywite Stone.

Plate 14. Example of
the vitrified stonework in
Amaru Machay cave, Peru.

**Plate 15.** Yurac Rumi (White Rock), Vilcabamba, Peru.
Photo by AgainErick.

**Plate 16.** Ica Stone showing men with strange
dinosaur-like creatures. Ica, Peru. Photo by David Woetzel.

Plate 17. Stone with fish-reptilian features, Fountainebleau, France. Photo by Bruno Teste.

Plate 18. Lion's Gate, Hattusha, Turkey. Photo by Bernard Gagnon.

Plates 19, 20, and 21. Asuka, Japan. Photos by z tanuki.

**Plate 22.** Ellora Caves, India. Photo by Saurabh Koravi.

**Plate 23.** Perperikon Water Reservoir, Bulgaria. Photo by Guido van Beurden.

**Plate 24.** Perperikon, Bulgaria. Photo by Ben Lee.

**Plate 25.** El Fuerte. Samaipata, Bolivia. Photo by Mhwater.

Plate 26. Samaipata, Bolivia. Photo by Dan Lundberg.

Plate 27. Tetzcotzinco, San Dieguito Xochimanca, Mexico.

However, Dorian was very spiritual, which was one of the reasons she was living at a Yogananda community—a place where sacred music was played every day.

According to her story, the Pleiadians conveyed to her the technique of intoning certain root sounds through the chakra system, as well as how to entrain them—which means to repeat a tone over and over again for about five minutes, focusing on the particular chakra and its color, and then work your way up to finish at the crown chakra. After taking good mental notes, she transcribed these instructions into a book and made a CD called *Sing the Body*, which was used in many retreat centers around the world.

After one of her healing sessions, Dorian told me that various temples situated on the Nile were in fact sound healing centers, and that each temple is tuned to a certain frequency. She said people would go to a particular temple associated with a particular type of healing that they needed to have done. I can imagine that for more holistic healing people would go on a pilgrimage to each site along the Nile—and who knows, maybe end at the Great Pyramid for the grand finale.

Is there anything to this amazing story that she told me? There is an historic account by a Greek traveler called Demetrius, circa 200 BCE, who gave a description of how the Egyptians used vowel sounds in their rituals:

> In Egypt, when priests sing hymns to the Gods they sing the seven vowels in due succession and the sound has such euphony that men listen to it instead of the flute and the lyre.[1]

And in the *Corpus Hermeticum,* whose authorship is traditionally attributed to the legendary Hermes Trismegistus, there is a reference to the Egyptians' use of sound as distinct from words. Within the *Corpus* there is a reference to a letter from Asklepios to King Amman. Asklepios says, "As for us, we do not use simple words but sounds all filled with power."[2]

As far as the physical temples themselves, how were they used in conjunction with sound? John Stuart Reid, an acoustic physics researcher and a respected authority in the field of cymatics (the creation of visual phenomena made with sound), says that singing or chanting in enclosed reverberation chambers would "enhance one's connection to spirit and optimize the choir and organ experience."

During his investigations into the sound properties in the King's Chamber in the Great Pyramid, Reid discovered that there was an acoustic coupling effect that centered right on the sarcophagus, a place were he believed that the pharaoh or initiates made communion with the spirit realm. The ancient engineers' stone of choice for the sarchophagus was granite with high quartz content—a material that would facilitate the reverberation of sound.

Besides sounds ability to facilitate higher states of consciousness and communion with the spiritual world, it was used for healing. Egyptian archaeologist and wisdomkeeper Abd'el Hakim Awyan backs up Dorian Carter's claim that the temples were used as amplifying chambers for the sounds that healed. Awyan said in the Gaia series *The Pyramid Code* that the twenty-two pyramids around the area called the "Band of Peace" are harmonic structures that used sound (in this case, sound and running water) to facilitate healing:

> Every chamber within the pyramid has a specific harmonic replicating the harmonics of the cavities of the human body. Sound healing techniques were then used to restore the patient's body to the correct harmonics.

Awyan also mentions that the step pyramid in Saqqara had a sort of hospital with an attendant physician. As transcribed on the site *egyptexperience*:

> I will take you now to the "hospital"—healing with sound—you see now—that line of construction—like three chambers—it's what's

left of the House of Spirit, and it's a healing system with the sound; it's a medical investigation table and the patient has the right to use any of the stairs, one on the right and one on the left, so he or she has to use his or her own "antenna" . . . to climb up there and choose the point where she [would] stand because each point is connected to a deep chamber—we have 22 of them, 11 each side, no ceiling— and when you go inside you see a niche where the physician put his head in the niche to see what is the matter with his patient lying on this table; and that works with sound, and the source is running water in a tunnel underneath here—there is a big map of tunnels running underneath here.[3]

Although anecdotal, John Stuart Reid also contends that he healed his lower back while doing cymatic sound experiments in the King's Chamber, which he attributes "to the resonant properties of the sar-cophagus [and] conjectures that the acoustic resonance was deliberately contrived by the Egyptian architects."[4]

Was sound healing common in the past? It seems so. Many, if not most, ancient and Indigenous cultures developed sound healing thera-pies, including the Aboriginal Australians with their didgeridoo, the Tibetans with their gongs and horns, the Shipibo with their icaros (medicine songs), and the Greeks with their flutes and lyres.[5] By using powerful sound devices, as well as chants and drums, probably at close proximity, the recipient could experience the desired effect. One can imagine that a temple specifically designed with selected high-density quartz rocks, set in acoustic chambers, and on sites with healthy telluric currents, might just give that extra boost to enhance healing.

What can be said about the temples and wakas in Peru? Is there any proof that sacred sites were used as sound healing centers? At Ollantaytambo, in the Sacred Valley, every guide knows that the Temple of the Ten Windows—a place with perfectly fitted Uran Pacha granite stones—has alcoves that, when sung into, or tapped by a rock, echo powerfully. You will frequently see guides and other individuals stick their heads into the niches to hum and intone vowels to find the perfect resonance.

Although the site is heavily damaged, possibly due to some ancient catastrophe as some researchers suggest, one can imagine that when this structure was fully covered—as evidence indicates via the opposing foundational stones' structures—it must have been a powerful sound chamber.

It is also believed that the Sillustani *chullpas* near Lake Titicaca could also be sound healing chambers, although the authorities say the tombs were designed to hold the mummified corpses of the highest Kolla nobility. That is most surely true, as they have found mummies and treasures within the chullpa structures, but, as we have seen in other cases of ancient sites, subsequent cultures repurpose older sites for their own rituals and uses. Many investigators say that they believe that these chullpas were originally designed to facilitate sound healing and altered states.

In a YouTube video posted by writer and researcher Hugh Newman, both he and author Brien Foerster maintain that the chullpas were originally designed as acoustic technology towers. Foerster comments in the video:

> So look at the possible theory that this was not a tomb originally for some ruler but was an acoustic generator. If you look at the shape it flares out from the bottom to the top, which doesn't make good building sense, but in the interior there was an entrance, and the interior was beehive shaped. The stone in the core is called andesite or diorite which is very hard, and it is quite densely packed in there with white clay from another area, so if you had tone in the inside, that tone could have been enhanced by the denseness of the diorite rock with some degree of the white clay acting as a type of insulation. Then you have an empty or hollow layer and then the structure is surrounded by basalt, a different stone, not as dense, and those divots in it could enhance the sound.[6]

Fig. 6.1. The author intones into one of the "windows"
at the Temple of the Ten Windows.
Photo by Francisco Carbajal.

Some of the Sillustani chullpas also display symbols that could represent the transformation of a person, either spiritually or physically. Though there is much damage to the site, one can see the image of a snake and a lizard carved on stones that made up the walls of two chullpas, animals that can represent both renewal for the shedding of skin (in the case of the snake) and regrowth (when a lizard grows its tail back after its loss). Of course, both these symbols could be used to represent healing or death (and rebirth) if they were originally designed as tombs; however, they may also be marks that indicate were earth energies are particularly strong. For instance, Freddy Silva, one of the foremost authorities on sacred sites, says that where snake motifs are depicted on megalithic sites it indicates telluric currents are present and concentrated.[7]

It is particularly interesting to note, as some of the Carnac menhirs mentioned in chapter four show carvings of serpents on them, which is something one sees on many sacred sites around the world. For example, if you walk around Cusco's old town, you will discover snake motifs everywhere on the walls of the old temples. They are also seen on Hanan Pacha monolith sites, most specifically in the Amaru Machay cave in the Moon Temple at the Sacsayhuaman complex. Is it possible that these snake symbols represent not only DNA molecules but also electromagnetic fields and sound frequencies—which may work together to enhance one's consciousness and stimulate one's health.

It seems like snake symbols have always been associated with health and medicine. We all have seen the caduceus symbol, composed of two snakes winding around a staff with a pair of wings near the top. It was the staff carried by Hermes, the god of communication and commerce in Greek mythology. Today this symbol is associated with the medical profession, along with the Rod of Asclepius, which is represented by one serpent entwined around a rod.

Although the Rod of Asclepius is the more accurate symbol for medicine and health care—as it is associated with the Greek god of

Fig. 6.2. Inner structure of a chullpa shows a beehive chamber.
Sillustani, Peru. See also color plate 11.

Fig. 6.3. Snake image carved on a stone at Sillustani, Peru.

Fig. 6.4. A vitrified snake at the Amaru Machay cave.
Sacsayhuaman, Peru.

healing, Asclepius—it seems that the caduceus has supplanted the rod in popular usage to represent health care. The caduceus more accurately represents communication and commerce, which one may argue is a more fitting symbol to represent today's health care industry. Many are not aware that this symbol was closely associated with alchemy, which, despite what many will tell you, is not solely about turning lead into gold; it is mainly a metaphor for transforming a base (lead) human being into a spiritualized and healthy (gold) being.

This is a very fitting symbol for transformation, as one cannot help but notice that the double-entwined snake has obvious similarities to the DNA molecule, as well as to the ayahuasca vine—a component of a very powerful medicine of the same name, which thousands of people take annually at retreat centers and ceremonies around the world. The caduceus's similarity to DNA is something that Jeremy Narby speculates about in *The Cosmic Serpent: DNA and the Origins of Knowledge*: "What if it were true that nature speaks in signs and that the secret to understanding its language consists in noticing similarities in shape or in form?"

Can there be anything more significant than the powerful and mysterious DNA molecule, the blueprint of life itself? To me this miracle molecule is confirmation of intelligent design by its intricate and complex programming nature. Here, Narby articulates the amazing functions of the DNA molecule:

When I started reading the literature of molecular biology, I was stunned by certain descriptions. Admittedly, I was on the lookout for anything unusual, as my investigation had led me to consider that DNA and its cellular machinery truly were an extremely sophisticated technology of cosmic origin. But as I pored over thousands of pages of biological texts, I discovered a world of science fiction that seemed to confirm my hypothesis. Proteins and enzymes were described as "miniature robots," ribosomes were "molecular computers," cells were "factories," DNA itself was a "text," a "program," a "language," or "data." One only had to do a literal reading of contemporary biology to reach shattering conclusions; yet most authors display a total lack of astonishment and seem to consider that life is merely "a normal physiochemical phenomenon."[8]

The power of DNA is even more surreal and fantastic if one realizes it is a processor that interprets the world around us and transforms mind stuff to materiality. In an opinion paper, "spiritual scientist" Linda Gadbois explains how DNA functions:

DNA is actually composed of a liquid crystalline substance that acts as a form of antenna, receiver, and transmitter of holographic information. It's constantly in the process of taking in information from its environment and the ether as signs, archetypes, and imagery and translating it into holograms. It operates predominantly out of radionics where whatever frequency it's tuned to, acts as a receiver for various forms of information within that same frequency that comes in as an acoustic wave that serves to form an electromagnetic field (EMF) as a holographic shape that's composed initially of subtle energy, which provides the blueprint or spatial mapping for constructing an exact replica as its material equivalent. Information inherent in the Ether (Akasha) always comes as a "pairing" or "wave coupling" (like the double helix) that contains both an acoustic sound and optical (visual) image as the geometric patterning inherent in the vibratory frequency.[9]

If Gadbois's observations about DNA are correct—that it acts as a receiver, transmitter, and processor of information from the environment, which facilitates generating holograms that eventually manifest, via the ether, in the material realm—then the aphorism "you are what you think" is much more meaningful than we can imagine. Haven't we heard this before? Think it, visualize it, and it shall be.

Regarding this idea that DNA was both a receiver and transmitter of information, it certainly signifies communication, which was Hermes's forté. Hermes was called the messenger of the gods; he was a psychopomp—a conductor of souls into the afterlife, able to move quickly and freely between the worlds of the mortal and the divine. These attributes sound a lot like the communication powers inherent in the DNA molecule, the basis of life itself.

If we were to take Hermes's image literally, might he represent a divine being that brought DNA to Earth? After all, there are many world legends that speak of godlike beings that brought seeds and plants to Earth and even developed genetically modified humans.* Not only did these gods bring seeds but also the knowledge of cultivation and civilization, which would also mean commerce—another area that Hermes was said to help facilitate.

Fig. 6.5. Hermes with his winged caduceus.

---

*As in Marduk's pronouncement in *Enuma Elish, The Sumerian Epic of Creation*, "Blood I will mass and cause bones to be. I will establish a savage, 'man' shall be his name. Verily, savage man I will create. He shall be charged with the service of the gods That they might be at ease! The ways of the gods I will artfully alter."

# SOUND:
# THE POWER TO HEAL OR DESTROY

Since we know that the background electromagnetism and radiation in our environment, as well as the frequency of our thoughts, can affect DNA, this brings up many fascinating and complicated questions that seem to be off the radar for most scientists and politicians. These issues, unaddressed, can have the most profound implications for life on this planet, especially at a time when we are blanketing our Earth in electromagnetic fields and strong radio frequencies, like 5G. We also have multiple generations of kids and adults obsessed with violent video games, movies, and porn. One has to wonder if we are actually manifesting sickness and conflict with these background frequencies, and the frequencies of our thoughts.

This idea that our thoughts have power to manifest our reality is backed up by the research of Masaru Emoto, author of the bestselling book *The Hidden Messages in Water*. Emoto discovered that water crystals changed their shapes when exposed to different sounds and thoughts.[10]

Emoto's research included experiments with verbal affirmations, music, thoughts, and prayers. He focused on positive affirmations like "I love you" as well as negative expressions like "you make me sick" and "I hate you," and directed these thoughts toward water in a Petri dish. When he analyzed the water under a microscope he noticed significant changes in the structure of the water, with the water treated to positive affirmations showing a beautiful crystalline structure, and the water subjected to the negative expressions showing malformed and ugly structures. This was also the case with music: the water exposed to Beethoven and Mozart demonstrated beautiful and complex crystal shapes, and the water exposed to heavy metal showed a discordant and ugly structure.

This research is significant because we know that the human body is about 65 percent water, and it is in every living tissue and cell in our body. If this water is responding to the thoughts and sounds in the environment, we can be certain that it is affecting ourselves and others too—for good or ill.

Because sound and thought are such potent forces operating in the world, and in our collective consciousness, shouldn't we be paying more attention to where we put our awareness, especially to what we choose to consume for entertainment?

What we do know is that ancient peoples, specifically those that lived in what the Greeks defined as the Golden Age, lived in a very different world than our present—one with less background radiation or "noise" that could confuse their sensitivity to natural frequencies in the environment. On top of this, they didn't have violent entertainment and fear-based news fed to them constantly via television and video games, things that would impinge on their psyche. They not only lived more simply, but also were more attuned to the rhythms and cycles of nature. Shifts in electromagnetic fields and telluric currents were probably picked up as one feels a faint wind on the skin, and sensing good spots to settle and cultivate food were intuitively known, especially by seeing the health of the land and animals. Keenly sensitive to the environment and with brains capable of rational thought, it is no wonder humanity thrived in and populated every corner of the Earth.

# 7

# Did Acoustic
# Levitation Move
# the Megaliths?

*If you want to find the secrets of the universe, think in
terms of energy, frequency and vibration.*

NIKOLA TESLA

One of the interesting theories promoted on websites and on
online forums that discuss megalithic work is that the ancients
used acoustic levitation to lift and move massive rocks. If you decide to
look into this subject, you are sure to come across the curious Dr. Jarl,
a Swedish doctor who came to Tibet in 1939 to treat a high lama in a
monastery, and during his stay claimed to witness such a levitation.

According to one version of the story, he ended up staying in Tibet
for a considerable amount of time and developed close relationships
with some of the Tibetan monks from the monastery. One day, one of
the monks invited him to a clearing near a tall cliff on top of which they
were constructing a stone wall. He noticed that, in the otherwise bar-
ren meadow, there was an enormous polished slab of rock with a bowl

shape carved in the middle of it. He also observed that the monks were guiding an ox dragging a large boulder, and when it got to the stone, the monks proceeded to put the boulder onto the concave rock. The monks then set up nineteen musical instruments—thirteen drums and six trumpets that were three meters in length—in a radiating 90-degree arc approximately sixty-three meters from the stone. Some monks then began to play the drums and blow the trumpets, while others, standing behind the instruments, started to chant. Although nothing happened at first, the rock eventually began to sway and lift. Hidden history researcher, David Wilcock, gives a description:

> When the stone was in position, the monk behind the small drum gave a signal to start the concert. The small drum had a very sharp sound and could be heard even with the other instruments making a terrible din. All the monks were singing and chanting a prayer, slowly increasing the tempo of this unbelievable noise. During the first four minutes, nothing happened; then as the speed of the drumming, and the noise, increased, the big stone block started to rock and sway, and suddenly it took off into the air with an increasing speed in the direction of the platform in front of the cave hole 250 meters high. After three minutes of ascent, it landed on the platform.[1]

Figure 7.1 on page 100 is a drawing by Henry Kjellson, a friend and associate of Dr. Jarl, which shows how the rock, the instruments, and the monks were oriented relative to the distances of the rock and cliff wall.

Dr. Jarl claims to have witnessed the monks moving five to six stones an hour with this method. In shock at what he was seeing, he thought he was hallucinating, or was under some kind of psychosis, so he ended up setting up a movie camera to film this miracle. It was said that he made two films of this incident, which his employer, an English scientific society, confiscated upon his return to Europe.

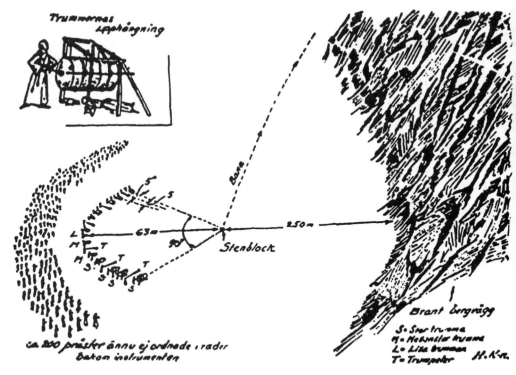

Fig. 7.1. Image by Henry Kjellson showing the method
used to levitate the stone.

The difficulty of finding more details about this amazing story is
noted in an online article by Bruce Cathie:

> I tried to find the original account that Dr. Jarl allegedly published
> in a German journal, as I thought it such a fascinating story, but if it
> ever really existed, today it seems flushed down the memory hole. It
> is also strange that I couldn't find a first name or any type of biogra-
> phy about him, but, like any enduring legend, his fame is kept alive
> on the internet with YouTube videos and on many websites dealing
> with lost technologies.[2]

Unfortunately, many websites that write about this story do not
mention Henry Kjellson, the civil engineer, flight manager, and author

who first championed Dr. Jarl and his story in his book *Försvunnen Teknik* (Lost Technology). I began to wonder: Was this Dr. Jarl even real? I discovered I was not the only one trying to get more details about the elusive Dr. Jarl; one Swedish investigator using the online name of "Hedvallen" was also curious about this story, and he started to do some research on his fellow countryman. Here is what he posted on the forum of Graham Hancock's website:

> Many times and for a lot of time I've been trying to find more information about Dr Jarl, was he even real? What is the source of the story? . . . So I found out that the source of the story about Dr. Jarl is originally coming from a Swedish book called "Försvunnen Teknik," translated to English as "Lost Technology" . . .

Hedvallen continues in his somewhat awkward English:

> I found that Henry Kjellson was a well known respected flight director with [a] master of science. He was born the 8 of august 1891 and died . . . in 1962. . . . He was the leading Flight Engineer for the Swedish Air Force, later during his career he became the leading Flight Director for the Swedish Air Force. All his life he was dedicated to and interested in ancient technology, spending a lot of his time traveling/researching ancient technology. He also participated in countless of seminars and lectures regarding the topic. It wasn't until after Henry's active career that he started publishing books and hosting his own seminars/lectures about his own findings.[3]

So, is it possible there never was a first-person account published by Dr. Jarl? It seems more likely that Kjellson was the eyewitness to the amazing feat and used the pseudonym of Dr. Jarl to hide his own identity. We can surmise this by looking at his obsessive interest in lost technologies, and because there is almost no credible evidence that Dr. Jarl existed. But why go through the trouble and deception to hide his identity? The only conceivable reason is that Kjellson used a pseudonym to divert attention from himself, perhaps for his own safety. After all, there are many accounts about scientists and engineers who have discovered—or rediscovered—advanced technology, and have seen their labs and offices raided by "Men in Black" who have confiscated their technologies and patents. Nikola Tesla was just one example of a scientist who had his work confiscated immediately after his death, work that disappeared from the public domain for decades.[4] There are also cases of individuals who disappeared or died suddenly right after they announced a discovery, especially when it had anything to do with free energy devices.[5]

Perhaps this account from Henry Kjellson was considered a national security threat and was hushed up by this "secret British scientific society" to keep the information out of the hands of those who could abuse this knowledge. After all, when this story was alleged to happen, in 1939, war was on the horizon. This kind of technology most surely would have been considered dangerous in the wrong hands, and this is possibly a reason that Kjellson (aka. Dr. Jarl) needed a pseudonym until 1961, when he felt it was safe to reveal his story.

This subterfuge seems plausible, as Kjellson's book mentions that the Tibetan monks could "walk on water, create materia from nothing, destroy materia into atoms, spawn houses with their mind, cut bread from one loaf of bread for eternity, turn water from ice," and so on.[6] Kjellson seemed aware that the monks had potentially dangerous powers.

So, what have we learned in the eighty-plus years since this event allegedly took place? Well, for one thing, scientists and researchers have now demonstrated in their labs that acoustic levitation is feasible, and, two, that humans are still probably not evolved enough to be trusted with these powers. However, maybe it is better if we leave questions of our ethical nature aside for the time being, and let's explore the new acoustic levitation technologies coming out of labs today.

## MODERN ACOUSTIC LEVITATION
## TECHNIQUES

Back in 2012, physicist Chris Benmore from the Argonne National Laboratory became an internet sensation when he demonstrated how two speakers that are precisely aligned can create standing waves that cancel out gravity, allowing drops of water and small objects to levitate. The feat of "magic" demonstrated via a YouTube video, immediately went viral and was later picked up by *Wired* and science blogs and magazines.[7] Today the video has nearly two million views.

Although this was a groundbreaking scientific discovery, Argonne's technology was very limited, as it could only suspend very small objects in a standing wave in a horizontal linear field—the objects couldn't move laterally or up and down, so its real-world applications were limited to laboratory diagnostic work. Today, the science of acoustic levitation has evolved, and researchers are lifting not only heavier objects, but have figured out how to stabilize and move them.

Another big advance in acoustic levitation science was revealed in 2018, when University of Bristol researchers announced a significant breakthrough in levitation science by figuring out a way to get larger objects to levitate without losing stability in an acoustic tractor beam array. Using ultrasonic waves set at a pitch of 40 kHz, they created rapidly fluctuated vortices set around a stable "silent core," which allowed objects that were more than twice the size of the wavelength to levitate, something that had never been done before. Prior to this scientists couldn't levitate objects that were larger than the wavelength without the objects spinning off uncontrollably. The scientists hope to build bigger and more powerful arrays to levitate larger items in the future.

Though the last two examples showed how it is possible to levitate simple and light objects like drops of liquid and a polystyrene sphere using sound, what about moving an object from one destination to another? Here too modern science is making some inroads. Asier Marzo from the Public University of Navarre, Spain, along with his colleagues, has developed a machine called LeviPrint, which uses a robot arm that can create very specific sound waves. The arm's movement and acoustic levitation abilities mean that it can carry components to assemble an object from them without touching any parts. In the video that the scientists created to demonstrate their invention you can see objects within the array moving up and down and to the sides with great stability.[9]

Every year we see more and more advancements to this technology, although scientists are nowhere close to figuring out how to move massive stones. Some recent discoveries may change this problem very quickly, though, with the astonishing discovery of the anti-gravitational properties of sound.

## SOUND AND ITS ANTI-GRAVITATIONAL PROPERTIES

In the paper "Gravitational Mass Carried by Sound Waves," scientists from the Center for Theoretical Physics at Columbia University explain how sound frequencies can cancel out gravity and move mass. The researchers found out that phonons (sound waves) are affected by gravity but in a highly unexpected way: instead of going down to the Earth, the phonons go upward. The scientists discovered that the phonons have mass, but it is a negative mass with negative gravity. As they explain in the introduction:

> It is usually said that sound waves do not transport mass. They carry momentum and energy, but it is an accepted fact that the net mass transported by a sound wave vanishes. Here, we question this "fact." A first indication that sound waves can carry a non-zero net mass is contained in the results of Ref. [1]: there, using an effective point-particle theory, it was shown that phonons in zero-temperature superfluids have an effective coupling to gravity, which depends solely on their energy and on the superfluid's equation of state. For ordinary equations of state, this coupling corresponds to a

negative effective gravitational mass: In the presence of an external gravitational field, such as that of Earth, a phonon's trajectory bends upwards..[10]

This is a truly astonishing discovery. If sound can cancel out gravity and move mass, it seems to give support to the notion that some people knew how to levitate and move massive stones with sound. After all, many oral traditions and myths relate how the ancients built their temples by levitating stones by chant and sound.[11]

Were the Tibetan monks mentioned earlier in this chapter aware of the unique principles of sound when they lifted these rocks? Could their orchestra composed of drums and horns angled at a ninety-degree angle, and some sixty-three meters away from the stone, have created that sweet spot to create a spinning vortex that helped them lift and guide the rock into place?

Looking at the Kjellson illustration of the monks moving stones (fig. 7.1, p. 100), it seems possible that the cliff wall could have acted as an amplifier and feedback loop for the sound waves, enhancing the spinning vortex properties as well. The rock also seems to be in the exact center between the monks and the cliff wall. Can this be an accident? Also, one sees that there were no humans in front of the large horns or drums, helping to minimize any damage to their bodies from the sound frequencies.

I am not aware of any research institution or group of individuals that have attempted to replicate what the monks did—that is, if they really did levitate stones, but I think it would be a great project to pursue for any acoustic scientists out there. Hint, hint.

## THE CURIOUS STONE BOWLS OF GIZA

What caught my attention about Kjellson's Tibetan story was that he mentioned that the stone used to levitate rocks was large—about one meter wide, and concave. I remember hearing about a similar story coming out of Egypt. It turns out that there are a series of huge lime-stone and quartz basins littered around the perimeter of the solar temple of King Nyuserre in Abu Ghorab, and a few researchers have speculated they were used for levitation purposes. However, this is not the accepted opinion of modern-day Egyptologists who say these basins were used as blood collectors after ritual sacrifices. (Similar stories are found here in Peru too, and this seems to be the go-to answer any time archaeologists need to explain what the purpose was for any basin or channel on a rock.)

However, there is a problem with this explanation, as there is no evidence of trace residual blood on the stones, and there are no holes on the bottom for drainage found in the stone basins.

One can, however, find evidence of holes on the top rim of these structures: the limestone basins had three holes on one side of the stone (I could not help but notice that this was at the same ninety-degree angle that the monks and their instruments were arranged around in Tibet), and the quartz basins bore holes on four sides, equally spaced around the rock. According to author and researcher, Alex Putney, who has studied these bowls extensively:

> The huge quartz basins have a borehole centered on each of the four sides of the square bases of the instruments, while the comparable limestone examples display three machine-drilled holes on just one side of the square blocks. The diameters of the bowls appear to be uniform, suggesting they were part of a large array that once surrounded the pyramids before being collected in groups by Egyptian authorities for present-day public display.

Putney goes on to say that the outer pyramid stones appear to be a geopolymer and they are composed of a strange admixture of opal CT, hydroxyl-apatite, and silico-aluminates, which would enhance the limestone's "natural capacity to convert all atmospheric acoustic energy into an electrical current within the crystals, inducing a strong

Fig 7.2. Possible levitation bowls near
the Great Pyramids in Egypt.
Photo from the Human Resonance website.

electromagnetic field around the pyramid structures and within their passages and chambers." With these modular basins surrounding the piezoelectric calcite and quartz crystals filled pyramids, they create a transducive capacity to focus and amplify acoustic waves. "Mechanical flexing occurs in the quartz and calcite crystals as a uniform structural deformation that generates standing waves within the stones' crystalline lattice, eventually building a strong electromagnetic field that allows acoustic levitation."[12]

I had to wonder: If these basins were used to levitate massive stones, how did these stones get to the launch pad in the first place? I found in my research that there was a tenth-century historian and geographer named Abul Hasan Ali Al-Mas'udi, who may give us a clue. In

Fig. 7.3. Modular shaped bowl limestone rocks most
likely were laid out in an array. Giza, Egypt.
Photo from the Human Reasonance website.

Mas'udi's 30-volume collection of texts called *The Meadows of Gold and Mines of Gems*, he relates a story that was told to him in his travels about how Egyptian priests levitated stone. He writes that they first put a "magic papyrus" with symbols on it underneath the stone. The priests then proceeded to strike the stone with a special metal rod causing the stone to levitate, and with a simple guiding nudge, the priests set the stone in the motion, guided to its destination by other metal rods set along the sides of a path.

If this story by Al-Mas'udi is true, this may have been how the stones got to the Giza plateau but it doesn't explain how they got incorporated in the pyramid structure. Possibly the giant stone bowls found all over the plateau today were once used to levitate stones to the great heights needed to construct the pyramid. Perhaps the bowls might have been concentrators of certain frequencies, and, because of their modular design, could be laid out in certain arrangements by the ancient engineers to allow the stones to move up and laterally to wherever they needed to go on the pyramid.

Alex Putney, however, has a slightly more exotic take on them—he believed that they were used to create a substance called "lightwater," He writes:

> Both the piezoelectric properties and the perfectly formed concavities of the large, ancient stone basins confirm their utility as precision instruments for acoustic levitation, and their cultural context informs us that water was being levitated . . . Longevity and cellular rejuvenation were imbued by drinking lightwater in the resonant infrasound environment of the pyramid chambers.

Putney believes that the water being absorbed into the pyramids' limestone provided a piezoelectric transduction of the infrasound resonance of the sun that aligned with the human heart at rest (1.45 hertz) and that the pyramids were used to broadcast those beneficial frequencies around the world.

> The high-walled enclosure, resembling a courtyard, contained energetic waters identified by the local Indigenous wisdom traditions as Lake Hathor. The lake waters were absorbed by the porous limestone of the pyramids, and provided direct electrical connection to the subterranean water table and thereby to the world's oceans. The pyramid texts of Saqqara describe this absorption of water within the stones in exact terms, stating that the pyramids' "foundations are the stones, the water." The hieroglyphic inscription on the obelisk at Abu Ghurab reads "Heart of the Sun" in reference to the pyramid network's piezoelectric transduction of the infrasound resonance of the sun, at the 1.45 Hz frequency of the human heart at rest. Were

the pyramids responsible for the regulation of global heartbeat patterns and weather patterns?[14]

These ideas bring up some of the concepts laid out in chapter four about how water, sun, and stone on top of an earth power spot may enhance beneficial electromagnetic fields or frequencies. One wonders if the sun-charged water flowing through high-quartz containing stones to the towers at Sacsayhuaman might have had a similar function. If pyramids and other sacred sites were used in this way, their builders must have been giants—if not in stature, then in their intellectual capacity to understand the energetic mysteries of the natural world and how to manipulate them as well.

# 8

# Proof of Geopolymers Used

*In geology, as in history, the material in hand remains silent if no questions are asked. The nature of these questions depends on the "school" to which the geologist belongs and on the objectivity of his investigations.*

R. W. VAN BEMMELEN

There has been an ongoing debate for many years—if not for centuries—about how the polygonal megaliths at Sacsayhuaman, and elsewhere, were created. If you want to see how interesting the debates can be, visit YouTube and type in "how were the walls of Sacsayhuaman created?" and read the replies below the videos. Sometimes the debate on these sites can be very technical, and at times quite contentious, as a few people seem to put their reputations on the line when promoting their favorite theory.

Though I don't think it is necessary to rehash the many interesting hypotheses out there—as they have been extensively explored by academics, as well as by many best-selling authors—I do think it is worthwhile to reexamine the geopolymer issue as today we have new forensic tools that can confirm anomalies in rock that would help us determine their composition and origin. These tools were not available when some of the most famous orthodox writers, like architect Vincent R. Lee ("The Building of Sacsayhuaman," 1986) and professor Jean-Pierre Protzen (*The Stones of Tiahuanaco: Architecture and Construction of an Andean Megalithic Center*, 1987) wrote their theories about how megalithic work was constructed. For instance, today scientists can confirm through electron microscopes (SEMs) and XRF analysis (X-ray fluorescence) whether rocks are quarried or reconstituted-stone based on the molecular structure and chemistry of the rocks sampled.

So, what exactly do I mean when using the term *geopolymer*? Although the definition of a geopolymer has various meanings, in the case of archaeological studies, it refers to various minerals reconstituted from natural sources into a re-agglomerated stone or cement that can be molded in its early state and harden over time. This unique attribute of geopolymers may give us a clue as to how Sacsayhuaman's colossal stone walls, and Pumapunku's massive andesite stones near Tiwanaku in Bolivia, were made.

In the case of Sacsayhuaman, it is believed that a team of Russian scientists who were asked to help analyze the site of Sacsayhuaman for the Ministry of Culture of Peru discovered geopolymers. The team was called in because the Ministry was in a crisis when workers at the Sacsayhuaman grounds noticed destructive processes taking place at the site: large cracks coming forth in the main walls, a shifting of the stone blocks, and recession of the walls. It was believed that such trends would be irreversible and potentially catastrophic if some kind of action wasn't immediately taken. Since Sacsayhuaman is one of the most significant "Inca" treasures in Peru, and one of the most visited sites, the Ministry had to do something, so they called in Geo & Asociados SRL to analyze the problem:

The selection of the company was not by accident as the experts of this research company possess the technology of georadar scanning, that was developed in the Russian institute VNIISMI, and which has no analogy in the world. The georadars of "Loza" series allow exploring the geologic structure of land till the level of 200 meters below the ground surface. Such georadar researches allow the experts of GPR Loza to detect the areas of high humidity, the fissures in rock formations, crust fractures, underground objects, etc.

The Russian team, headed by N. Berdnikov and O. Kozlova, using their powerful georadar, found significant structural issues lying underneath Sacsayhuaman's walls. This was due to the fissured rocky soil which was used for water basin drainage, which could lead to " . . . uncontrollable local movement of ground waters under the wall's foundation [which] will lead to the washout of the easily soluble fractions of the top layer of soil and to the loss of the carrying capacity of the wall's foundation."[1]

They also did analysis of the rock walls at the site for preservation purposes, and discovered something unexpected and paradigm-shattering in its implications. In a presentation for the Ministry of Culture of Peru, the scientific team presented evidence that the stones forming the walls at Sacsayhuaman had significant differences from the rock found at the quarries, indicating they were somehow reconstituted.[2]

The Russian team used optical microscopy, as well as XRF analysis (X-ray fluorescence), and determined that the walls were composed of microcrystalline limestone that contained no organic skeletal fragments, whereas all of the samples from the quarry had clear signs of organic skeletal remains, typical for natural limestone rocks.

Most interestingly, their analysis of the chemical makeup of both the stones at the quarry and the megalithic stones showed that the mineral composition was nearly identical, which seems to indicate that

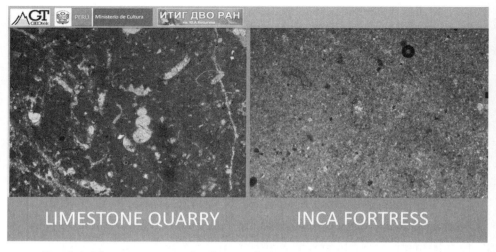

Fig. 8.1. The quarry sample shows obvious organic structures that are missing in the stones and the monument.
Source: Peru Ministry of Culture.

the quarry most likely was the source for the stones for the megalithic walls—however, in a reconstituted state. The Russian team seemed to think that the rocks at the walls were originally of a moldable consistency, which would explain their ability to shape perfectly into existing shapes or molds as is apparent in polygonal megalithic work.

They also said they believed the Hanan Pacha monoliths formed at other places on the grounds at Sacsayhuaman were reconstituted plasticine limestone that was worked over a harder andesite foundation.

The team mentioned in the presentation that more research was needed; however, it is not clear if the Ministry of Culture decided to take them up on this offer, as there was some resistance to this plasticine rock hypothesis in the room. This is not surprising, because it would seem to contradict years of research by some of the leading academics in the field of geology and archaeology who had studied the site. One commentator at the presentation said: "Seemingly the facts presented here today do not fit into our perception of reality. This always leads some people to come up with some supernatural origins of phenomena."

I am not sure why evidence of geopolymer use implies that there must be a supernatural origin, because today the use of geopolymers in industry, and in the arts, is well known. It is used in many applications including for building material, in ceramics, and in sculpture. Maybe this geopolymer hypothesis is a threat to some who want to uphold the carefully crafted trope that the Incas built Sacsayhuaman solely with quarried stone that was carried to the site.

A subsequent commentator at the presentation said that the rocks at Sacsayhuaman couldn't be geopolymers because the tops of the stones weren't flat. Apparently he believed that geopolymers must have the viscosity of oil or paint and be poured; however, the Russian geologist in the presentation never said anything about the viscosity of the geopolymer used. As anyone who has ever used polymer clays knows, such materials can mold to any shape. Artists around the world use them to do incredibly detailed sculptures of human anatomy and organic forms, and none of them are limited to molds to hold their shape until hardened. The angled and irregular tops of the stones used in the walls at Sacsayhuaman could have been sculpted in sectional forms with a heavier, viscous clay. Starting from the bottom to the top, after one section hardened, another section of soft polymer could be put on top of the previous hardened stone to fit perfectly in place. Over time, during the dry and hot, sunny days and freezing nights, so typical of the climate in the Andes, these polymer sections could have cured and hardened the stones that we see today.

Even though the Russians presented some compelling evidence to the Ministry of Culture, and to the other scientists in attendance, I can understand the resistance in the room to geopolymers being used. This information flies counter to conventional wisdom as well as the countless studies and books written by researchers and academics who worked tirelessly for decades trying to explain how the ancients created these monoliths from quarried rock, stone, and copper tools and brute strength. If the Russian scientists' premise were proven right, there

Fig. 8.2. An example of the precision and
scale of the stones and Sacsayhuaman.

would have to be serious reconsideration of how Sacsayhuman was
built—and by whom.

## GEOPOLYMERS MAKE SENSE

Another problem with the official story about Sacsayhuaman and other
megalithic sites is that there is no evidence of how they moved the massive boulders, some weighing more than three hundred tons, to the
site itself. As architect Vincent Lee mentions in an interview with Dr.
David Miano, "The only evidence they have of the Inca moving stones
comes from a drawing in a book by Guaman Pomo de Ayala called
*A Letter to a King*, in which he shows a picture of stone being dragged
directly on the ground by a bunch of guys with ropes tied around the
stone, and their supervisor standing on the stone." Even Lee admits
"this seems a little fanciful when you consider the size of the stones
used at Sacsayhuaman."[3]

Also, the only report that we have from Chroniclers about the Inca moving massive stones comes from Garcilaso de la Vega in his *Royal Commentary of the Incas*. He mentions an account of how an Inca king had tried to emulate the achievement of his predecessors at Sacsayhuaman by attempting to transport just one massive rock from miles away to the fortification. Unfortunately, it was an unmitigated disaster. De la Vega writes:

> This boulder was hauled across the mountain by more than twenty thousand Indians, going up and down very steep hills, and that, at a certain spot, it fell from their hands over a precipice, crushing more than three thousand men.[4]

If the Inca had such a problem with just one massive stone, how could they have carried the thousands that it would have taken to build Sacsayhuman's walls? As anyone can see who visits Sacsayhuaman, the landscape is quite hilly, and there are rough outcrops of andesite and limestone, as well as water basins and creeks, everywhere. These obstructions would be incredible barriers to such an endeavor, even if the men could conceivably pull the stone just with ropes and brute strength.

In the case of Ollantaytambo, another megalithic site in the Cusco region, which Vincent Lee also examined extensively, the ground is very steep and treacherous. Lee's explanation that the massive stones, some weighing hundreds of tons each, could have been dragged by ropes from the high mountain quarry six kilometers away—down the steep mountain ravine, ferried over the Vilcanota River, and then dragged up an incredibly steep mountain to the megalith area of the site—is in my opinion not credible. I've visited this site many times while living here in the Sacred Valley, and I just can't see how this could have been done. And I am not the only one. Even the official travel site of Peru seems dubious about how the stones got there intact; they even seem confused about who actually created the site! From their website: "The Ollantaytambo temple is an impressive architectural ensemble. It is located at 2,792 meters of altitude and is 3,500 years old." However, just two paragraphs below this statement we read that it is one of the great wonders of Incan architecture:

> One of the most surprising details of Ollantaytambo is that the rocks found in the complex are perfectly polished, have impeccable cuts and are intact, which means that the builders were able to lift the stones and transport them without suffering any damage. Which is quite a feat, because the fortress is built on a very steep slope. Without a doubt, Ollantaytambo is one of the great wonders of Inca architecture that until this day generates doubts and questions, many of them still unanswered.

Yes, I have some doubts and unanswered questions! From all authoritative accounts, the Incan empire only lasted about a hundred years, from 1438 to 1533, so I am not sure how the writer could have missed this anomaly in the timeline. It doesn't help either that there is no explanation as to where the 3,500-year-old number came from, but maybe this is a clue: under the photo of Ollantaytambo stonework is the caption: "According to researchers, this complex has its origins in the Aymara culture."[5]

Okay, so which is it? Is the temple complex of Ollantaytambo an example of Aymara architecture (an Andean/Antiplano culture mainly in the Lake Titicaca region of Peru) or Incan architecture? Perhaps this is a case of the Incas assimilating the building techniques of the Aymara people? But that is also problematic, because the Aymara aren't known as megalithic builders.

Maybe this confusion stems from the fact that the Incas were inheritors of advanced stone-building techniques and hydraulic engineering from the many other cultures they conquered, and many of these cultures go considerably back in time. Tiwanaku (sometimes spelled

Fig. 8.3. The author looking at a scoop mark on a
megalithic stone at Ollantaytambo.
Photo by Francisco Carbajal.

Tiahuanaco) and its sister site adjacent to it, Pumapunku, are examples of this much older culture. One of the greatest scholars on Tiwanaku, Arthur Posnansky, believed that site was more than 15,000 years old based on astronomical measurements of the main temple.[6]

So, once again, can we really attribute these amazing megalithic sites to the ancestors of the Aymara or Tiwanakans, more known for beautiful pottery and textiles than megalithic work? Even the locals, when you ask them, seem doubtful as to who built them, and Chroniclers at the time of the Inca stated that the locals mentioned that these buildings were already ancient ruins way before their ancestors arrived in the area.

The Peru travel website seems to reflect some of the overall murkiness that shrouds the provenance of ancient sites like Tiwanaku, Sacsayhuaman, and Ollantaytambo. However, maybe there is hope! It seems that we may have a solution to the dating issues, and who built them, with the recent discoveries of carbon-based organic matter—in rock!

## ORGANIC MATTER FOUND IN GEOPOLYMER STONES

A relatively recent study from the Geopolymer Institute and Universidad Catolica San Pablo in Arequipa, Peru, led by Joseph Davidovits, has demonstrated that the incredibly precise megaliths at Tiwanaku and Pumapunku are composite geopolymers. Most significantly, they found organic matter in them, which could lead to radiocarbon testing and could, hopefully, assign relative dates to the stones.

This team was the first ever to analyze the massive red sandstone terraces (the biggest being 180 tons) and smaller andesite stones from the Pumapunku site under an electron microscope, and they discovered the artificial nature of the stones. They also took samples from local geological resources and found significant differences between the natural stone and the stone from the monument.

Regarding the four red sandstone blocks that are used for the platforms at Pumapunku, they found that none of the possible geological sources corresponded to the stones of the archaeological monuments. In addition, the local stone is friable and small in size and the quarries that were available could not provide massive blocks of ten meters long. The scientists also "discovered under the electron microscope that the red sandstone of Pumapunku cannot come from the region because it contains elements, such as sodium carbonate, not found in the local geology."

Another clue that the rocks were not quarried is that the andesite samples they found have carbon-based organic matter within them, which does not exist in volcanic rock since it is formed under extremely high heat. Any organic material in the rock would have been vaporized. The organic element of carboxylic acids, according to the scientists, could only have been added by humans.[7]

This reminds me of old Andean folklore and accounts by Chroniclers that some kind of organic material was once used to soften stone, and one of these Chroniclers, Father Jorge Lira, a Peruvian priest, allegedly carried out a experiment using a red-plant concoction called *jotcha* to prove it.[8] Though the accounts say Lira could soften stone, it turns out that he was only partly successful as he could not harden the stone again once the paste was applied. It is recorded that the magical plant formulation was a mixture of this red plant material (other names are *kechuca, puno punco, quebrantahuesos,* or bone-breaker Andean ephedra), and other plants of an unknown nature. Supposedly the natives discovered its stone liquefying properties by observing the Pito woodpecker (*Colaptus Pitius*), who by means of its saliva had fermented the plant juice in it, and could drill stones with its beak.

Davidovits also believes that it was possible the Tiwanakan culture of 1400 years ago could have developed the necessary skills to manufacture these geopolymer stones by observing the natural world and by experimenting with materials around him:

Fig. 8.4 Pumapunku stonework, Bolivia.
See also color plate 12.

What is this technology mastered by the Tiwanakans? Artificial stones were formed as cement. But, it is not modern cement, it is naturally-forming geological cement obtained by geosynthesis. For this, they took naturally friable and eroded rock like red sandstone from the nearby mountain, on the one hand, and on the other hand, unconsolidated volcanic tuff from the nearby Cerro Kapia volcano in Peru to form andesite. They created cement from clay (the same red clay that Tiwuanakans used for pottery) and sodium carbonate salts from Laguna Cachi in the Altiplano Desert to the south, to form red sandstone. For gray andesite, they invented an organo-mineral binder based on natural organic acids extracted from local plants and other natural reagents. This cement was then poured into molds and hardened for a few months. Without a thorough knowledge of geopolymer chemistry, which studies the formation of these rocks by geosynthesis, it is difficult to recognize the artificial nature of the stones. This chemistry is not a difficult science to master. It is an extension of the knowledge of Tiwanakans in ceramics, mineral binders, pigments and above all an excellent knowledge of their environment. Without the selection of good raw materials, these extraordinary monuments could not have been created 1400 years ago.[9]

Though I think it is a stretch to claim that the Tiwananku people, who were known for beautiful pottery and textiles, built the massively complex sites of Tiwanaku and Pumapunku, I think it might clear things up if we had some solid radiocarbon dating from the organic material *within* the andesite stones—and not just reference objects left at the site, which could have been left by any culture that may have visited these sites after the fact—to confirm these dates. If the rocks themselves could be carbon-14 dated, that would resolve a lot of questions about when Tiwanaku and Pumapunku were actually built, and possibly by whom.

After an email exchange with Professor Davidovits in August 2022, I found out that there was no radiocarbon testing on the organic matter in andesite stones. He said it was because they never made it back to the site.

## THE ENIGMATIC SAYWITE STONE

There is also another site that seems to prove the fact that geopolymers were used in its creation. The Saywite Stone is a large monolith about thirty minutes outside of the city of Abancay, and about three hours out of Cusco. It is probably one of the most interesting, though less frequently visited, sites in Peru. The monolith is covered with more than two hundred geometric and zoomorphic figures, including reptiles, frogs, and felines, and has numerous terraces, ponds, tunnels, water basins, and channels over its upper face.

The function and purpose of the rock is not universally agreed upon, researcher Arlan Andrews Sr. believes "the monolith was used as a scale model to design, develop, test, and document the water flow for public water projects, and to teach ancient engineers and technicians the concepts and practices required."[10] One of the more interesting aspects to the stone is that it looks to be made of a geopolymer. According to Andrews, "The rock was 'edited' several times, with new material, either altering the paths of the water or adding routes altogether."[11]

Since all stonemasons and architects know that the carving of stone is a subtractive process—a pounding and chipping away of excess stone by various tools—how does the Saywite Stone fall into a category of a stone sculpture if it was created by adding material? It must be a geopolymer as well.

Furthermore, by looking at the rock you can see telltale signs that it was molded, including its lower section, which shows no indications of tool marks. It looks as if someone first put geopolymer material in a pool, hardened it, and started working, layer by layer, on top of the mold. It even has holes surrounding the edge—one can imagine

Fig. 8.5. The Saywite Stone shows evidence that
geopolymers were used.

Fig. 8.6. A detail of the Saywite Stone.
See also color plate 13.

that this is how they removed the rock from the mold after it hardened, though others have suggested the holes are canals for water flow. Perhaps they were used for both purposes.

I also believe that the geopolymer issue may explain the phenomenon of precise drill holes, fingerlike impressions, and thin cut marks often seen on megalithic and monolithic stones throughout Peru. These would be impossible to do with bronze tools and pounding stones, which the Inca and Wari used to shape stone. It certainly would be much easier to create a hole or fine canal in softer material than on solid hard stone. I am not saying with certainty that this was how the work was done; however, it seems logical.

## THE EGYPTIAN CASING STONES

It turns out that the same Professor Joseph Davidovits who discovered the organic material in the andesite stones at Tiwanaku also made the case that the stones at the pyramids were a very early form of concrete created using a mixture of limestone, clay, lime, and water.

Professor Michel Barsoum of the Department of Materials Science and Engineering at Drexel University remembers the day he got a phone call from a colleague of Davidovits who suggested that Davidovits believed that the casing stones that covered the pyramids were a geopolymer. Though originally skeptical of the claim, Barsoum knew he could prove it "with just a few hours of electron microscopy."

As a consequence of that short phone call, Barsoum embarked on a five-year odyssey with graduate student Adrish Ganguly and Gilles Hug, a colleague from France, to find the truth.

A year and a half later and after extensive scanning electron microscope (SEM) observations and other testing, Barsoum found that the tiniest structures within the inner and outer casing stones were consistent with a reconstituted limestone and that the "cement binding the limestone aggregate was either silicon dioxide (the building block of quartz) or a calcium and magnesium-rich silicate mineral."

The team also discovered that the stones also had a high water content which was unusual for the natural limestone found at the Giza plateau, which is normally dry, and that both the inner and outer casing stones demonstrated amorphous atom structures without the usual arrays and structures that are almost always present in natural limestone.

Silicon dioxide nanoscale spheres (with diameters only billionths of a meter across) was also discovered by Barsoum and another of his graduate students, Aaron Sakulich, in one of the samples, which further confirms that these blocks are not natural limestone.

One thing these discoveries indicated is that the ancients not only had advanced skills in chemistry but advanced intuition too. It reminds me of the stories I heard about how people in the jungles of South America could have figured out that two plants, in a forest of tens of thousands of plants, could be combined to form the powerful brew of ayahuasca. It seems to me that this very intuition and insight into nature must have been applied as well to make these complex geopolymers. Maybe "this chemistry is not too difficult to master," as Professor Joseph Davidovits says, but it is another thing to have the insight to know how to mix these ingredients in the first place.

■ ■ ■

In conclusion, I think that the proof that geopolymers were used in the making of megalithic and monolithic works should change the conversation about how these structures were built, and may give us clues as to who built them, especially if we can get good radiocarbon dating samples from the actual rocks themselves. Also, the making of geopolymer stones—in situ—would be infinitely easier and more logical than cutting and hauling massive megalithic stones over rough terrain and Andean peaks, saving time, energy, and probably countless lives. If anyone is concerned that this somehow diminishes the legacy of the ancients as incredible builders, I would just say the opposite—this may be one of the most incredible engineering feats of all time.

# 9

# Evidence
# of Vitrification

*There are two ways of spreading light,*
*to be the candle or the mirror that reflects it.*

EDITH WHARTON

If one walks around the old town of Cusco, especially around the Koricancha area and Loreto Street, you may notice that there is a sheen that comes off the ancient stone walls, mainly seen on the borders where one rock meets another. And if you happened to do a night walk during a full moon, or used a flashlight to light your way, you would notice that these areas reflect a bright white light. If you were to touch these areas, you would notice how smooth and glossy they are to the touch, very unlike the rest of the rock.

This phenomenon is not only seen on Uran Pacha walls in the city of Cusco, but is also seen in Hanan Pacha work as well, with incredible examples seen in the cave of Amaru Machay at Lacco (also known as Templo de la Luna, or the Moon Temple), and in the Cheqtaqaqa, Teteqaqa huacas in the foothills around Sacsayhauman.

So, what is going on here? According to Alfredo Gamarra this is an example of vitrification, which is the use of high heat to change the molecular structure of stone. Vitrification is, essentially, the process of transforming any substance into glass. It happens when the materials in question are heated to a point at which they turn into liquid and then, when rapidly cooled, turn into a solid. Some of the effects of vitrification are a mirror-like, glossy surface with evidence of discoloration, as well as demonstrable light refraction and diffusion from the vitrified areas. One can also frequently see that there is a skin or surface layer on the rock, especially where areas on the surface have degraded over time.

Fig. 9.1. Example of vitrified rock at
Cheqtaqaqa, Cusco, Peru. Photo by Francisco Carbajal.

Conventional archaeologists say that this is an example of polishing techniques using sand and water, if they mention this phenomenon at all. However, this seems highly improbable when you see how the vitrified parts of the stone are sometimes in very small areas and at ninety degree angles, and frequently skip over rough areas on the same block, something highly unlikely to happen if a human were polishing the rock. There is also the molecular analysis of the rock itself, which shows evidence of a chemical change on its surface layer, something that couldn't happen with polishing techniques. Therefore, it seems there is enough evidence today to say that these rocks were subject to intense heat in order to cause this structural change.

However, it seems that it was not just heat alone that caused this phenomenon. There does seem to be evidence that a ceramic paste was added to the surface of the rock, and later it was subjected to high heat to form a vitrified glaze.

In a 2011 article written by Jan Peter de Jong and Christopher Jordan, the authors present compelling evidence, in the form of high-resolution microscopic images and spectral analysis, that a vitrified sample of rock from the Patallacta waka in Cusco had a glaze applied to it. The glaze's chemistry shows high levels of silicon along with aluminum and magnesium, levels that are significantly higher than in the non-vitrified body of the limestone rock. Also, they found double the amount of oxygen in the glazed sample. They write in regard to their finding's significance:

> The Silicon, Aluminium and Magnesium seem to indicate that a material was added to the surface of the stone. The oxygen may have been part of this matter or it may have been introduced as part of oxidation during an aerobic heating process. This could have been during the formation of silicate, $SiO2$.

The authors found that the glaze on this sample was almost identical to the glazes seen on ancient pottery, specifically ceramic pottery pieces from Catamarca, Argentina.

If an antique ceramic sample is compared to the spectra of the glaze above there is little to separate the two. In the paper X-Ray Techniques Applied to Surface Paintings of Ceramic Pottery Pieces

From Aguada Culture (Catamarca, Argentina) there are several comparable results. The samples are from pottery pieces from Argentina so an exact match is unlikely. These researchers tested a variety of different colored samples from Argentine pottery shards, which had residual gold leaf on the surface. The spectra are surprisingly similar if the gold leaf is ignored along with the Manganese (Mn) and Iron (Fe). The latter two elements have oxides that are common colorants in ceramic pastes. This is the source of the various colors in their research paper. The key constituents Silicon, Aluminum, Magnesium, Carbon and Oxygen are present in the same ratios.[1]

So it seems the ancient stone builders had an understanding of applied ceramics techniques that are commonly used on pottery, which isn't surprising looking at the rich history of ceramic work here in Peru. However, what is truly the most perplexing thing about this vitrification process found in the stones in Peru is that this effect is seen on massive natural rocks, as well as inside and outside of caves, which leaves the essential tool for ceramic work—the furnace or kiln—out of the question. So how could the ancients have created heat hot enough to create a glaze in open-air environments? We don't know the answer to that question, and all modern-day attempts to replicate the same results on large surfaces in the open air have failed to generate the heat necessary to vitrify the rocks. Because of this mystery, many speculate that the ancients must have had some advanced technology.

This is where the discussion turns to lasers, ultrasound waves, or focused and concentrated sunlight using mirrors. The latter theory was briefly proposed by Ivan Watkins, professor of geology at St. Cloud University in Minnesota in a 1990 paper on fine Inca workmanship. He writes:

> The rock surfaces on Inca stones are similar to those that have been thermally disaggregated. Indeed, some of the slick surfaces on the

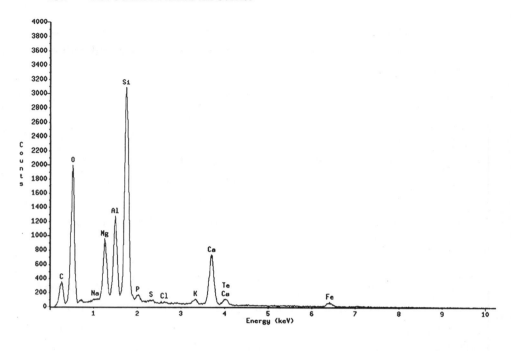

Fig. 9.2. Spectral analysis of surface layer of vitrified stones.
Image courtesy of Jan Peter de Jong.

Inca building stones are glazed, so it becomes apparent that the Incas must have used thermal disaggregation.[2]

Watkins suggests that the vitrification could have been done using large parabolic gold bowls like the ones that he discovered in a Cusco museum, bowls that could have been used to concentrate and focus the sun's rays. However, as de Jong and Jordan suggest, many of the vitrified samples are in caves that are quite deep and away from sunlight, so it seems improbable that sunlight reflected through mirrors could create the high heat needed to melt an applied glaze. For this reason they suggest that some other technology must have been used.

Fig. 9.3. Example of the vitrified stonework in Amaru Machay cave, Peru. See also color plate 14.

It does seem possible that the caves themselves might have been set on fire sometime in the past to create the glaze, but it doesn't explain how vitrification only shows on borders in the fitted stones in the walls in Cusco or on certain surfaces in the caves.

As to what heating tool was used to soften rock and melt glazes, it is still a mystery, and many theories have been bandied about. But there are no definite conclusions as to how the ancients did this.

Maybe the more important question we can ask is: Why did the ancients do vitrification at all? Why was it so important for them to vitrify the ledges and ridges in tunnel complexes or on *sillas* (thrones) on wakas, or in many cave chambers? Was there some characteristic in the glaze's property that was significant to the builders? Is there something about the chemistry of the glazed rock that imparts some energetic properties, properties that may facilitate electromagnetic fields and higher states of consciousness?

I have noticed that the more extensive use of vitrification seems to be done in caves in the Sascayhuaman area, which look to me like they were used for ceremonial purposes. If you notice the cave system of Amaru Machay, at the Temple of the Moon, you will see that almost the entire cave shows evidence of vitrification. The same thing is seen at Cheqtaqaqa and at Q'enko in the underground chambers.

Although I am not a chemist, I do know that silicon is a semiconductor. I also noticed that magnesium and aluminum were shown as components in the glaze on the vitrified rock under chemical analysis, and that these three substances are particularly good conductors of electricity. Scientist Jim Clark explains why these elements are so significant:

Sodium, magnesium and aluminum are all good conductors of electricity. Conductivity increases as you go from sodium to magnesium to aluminium. Silicon is a semiconductor. The three metals, of course, conduct electricity because the delocalised electrons (the "sea of electrons") are free to move throughout the solid or the liquid metal.

Clark also mentions how these three elements, when combined to melting points, can create a sea of charged atoms:

Melting and boiling points rise across the three metals because of the increasing strength of the metallic bonds. The number of electrons with each atom can contribute to the delocalised "sea of electrons" increases. The atoms also get smaller and have more protons as you go from sodium to magnesium to aluminium. The attractions and therefore the melting and boiling points increase because:

> The nuclei of the atoms are getting more positively charged.
> The "sea" is getting more negatively charged.
> The "sea" is getting progressively nearer to the nuclei and so more strongly attracted.[3]

Here we notice that when the metallic elements are heated to their chemical melting points they contribute to a "sea of electrons." Can it be a coincidence that the vitrification glaze in the Cheqtaqaqa rock sample is composed of the same elements known to be good conductors of energy? And that when these elements are heated to such a degree (the high heat of vitrification), their atomic bonds merge to create a sea of negative and positively charged electrons?

■ ■ ■

In conclusion, to me it seems very likely to me that the glazes in sacred sites may have been used to enhance electromagnetic fields to perhaps be used for altered states, healing, and perhaps communication.

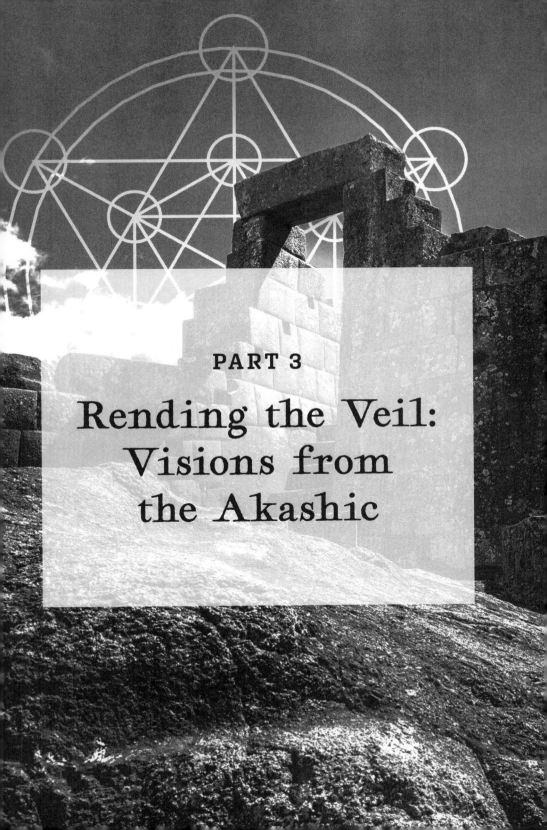

PART 3

# Rending the Veil:
# Visions from
# the Akashic

# 10

# The Viewers:
# Steiner, Blavatsky, and
# Subramuniya

*There is no higher religion than the truth.*

H. P. BLAVATSKY

I n this section I venture to explore the visions of famous clair-voyants who have peered into the Akashic Records to reveal humanity's early cosmogony. I have decided to delve into this shad-owy realm for the very reason that since there is nothing written in the historical record that would shine light onto the strange Hanan Pacha monoliths, which seem as if created by a different mind and race than our own, I thought it incumbent on me to explore other areas of perception.

At this juncture, we realize that because we can never verify human-ity's early past to the degree that empirical science would like—minus the hard evidence of tools, engineering, plans, or written history—we can either resign ourselves (by saying this subject will always be a mys-tery until hard evidence has materialized), or we can say that maybe the clairvoyants can provide some answers to these mysteries. Lacking a time machine, this may be our best shot at understanding what happened in the far past.

Let us look at what psychics have to say about early humans and how this could relate back to our question of who built the ancient monoliths and megaliths. As always, if this area of exploration doesn't appeal to you, please feel free to skip this chapter.

## RUDOLF STEINER:
## A MAN BETWEEN TWO WORLDS

Rudolf Steiner was a renaissance man born in the twentieth century, who is still highly regarded and influential today. Unlike most intellectuals and academics of his day, his contributions to society weren't just theoretical but practical. He designed the educational theories and curriculum for Waldorf Schools (called Steiner Schools in Europe),

Fig. 10.1. Rudolf Steiner in 1905.

which were based on a holistic, age-specific curriculum to develop a child's intellect and practical skills, as well as to foster their creativity and imagination. Today his biodynamic agricultural practices, one of the two pillars of the modern organic farming movement, are widely practiced around the world.

Steiner was also a prolific writer and lecturer who wrote forty books, including essays, plays, and an autobiography. He lectured on almost every imaginable theme, including art, natural science, medicine, literature, philosophy, and economics and education and agricultural practices.

It is good to spell out just how important and respected Rudolf Steiner was—and continues to be around the world as his critics often dismiss him as a charlatan because of his esoteric beliefs. However, just because the material-rationalist mind of the critic is not capable of understanding him—or all that willing to, for that matter—it does not in any way discredit what Steiner has to say about what he calls "supersensible" worlds. In fact, if we are to take Steiner as a trustworthy individual, as millions around the world do, then we should perhaps take as credible his views of humanity's past.

Steiner could always see beyond the veil of what can be observed with the five senses, and explore other dimensions of reality. For more than half his life he kept his psychic abilities under wraps because he felt it was necessary for someone with his abilities to be grounded in the scientific practices of the day. He often publicly commented on the frivolous and harmful practices of esotericists for their parlor acts, which he felt did more to harm supernatural investigation than benefit it. It was only much later in his life that Steiner started to integrate a more holistic approach that included spiritual matters into education:

From 1900, till his death in 1925, Steiner articulated an ongoing stream of 'experiences of the spiritual world'- experiences he said had touched him from an early age on. Steiner sought to apply all his training in mathematics, science, and philosophy in order to produce rigorous, intersubjectively testable presentations of those experiences. He also sought to bring a consciousness of spiritual life and non-physical beings into many practical domains—medicine, education, science, architecture, special education, social reform, agriculture, drama, among others. Steiner held that non-physical beings were in everything, and that through freely chosen ethical disciplines and meditative training, anyone could develop the ability to experience such beings, and thus be strengthened for creative and loving work in the world.[1]

Because Steiner could read the Akashic Records, and was deeply interested in the topic of human evolution, he wrote extensively on the sights he witnessed there. His lectures and writings on the lost continents of Lemuria and Atlantis were based on his observations from this other dimension.

If you are unfamiliar with what the Akashic Records are, Edgar Cayce, a popular American psychic and medium who popularized the Records, describes them as such:

The Akashic Records, or "The Book of Life," can be equated to the Universe's super-computer system. It is this system that acts as the central storehouse of all information for every individual who has ever lived upon the earth. More than just a reservoir of events, the Akashic Records contain every deed, word, feeling, thought, and intent that has ever occurred at any time in the history of the world. Much more than simply a memory storehouse, however, these Akashic Records are interactive in that they have a tremendous influence upon our everyday lives, our relationships, our feelings and belief systems, and the potential realities we draw toward us. . . . The Akashic Records contain the entire history of every soul since the dawn of Creation. These records connect each one of us to one another.[2]

If the Akashic records seem a bit farfetched to you, let's look at what is known and written about them, so we understand that this isn't some science fiction construct. According to the Akashic Studies Australia website, the Akashic records were known and consulted in ancient cultures in the past:

> Almost every culture has acknowledged the existence of the Akashic Records, including the Greeks, Assyrians, Babylonians, Egyptians, and more. The Akashic Records is not a religion, yet we find it mentioned in many sacred texts including the Christian Bible, the Hebrew Bible Tanakh, and the Qu'ran and even in Buddhism. The records or The Book of Life in the Christian Bible (Psalm 69:28, Philippians 4:3, Revelation 3:5, 13:8, 17:8, 20:12, 20:15 and Revelation 21:27) are described as being in a non-physical plane described as a library.
>
> In Tibet, ancient Tibetan scrolls and Buddhist writings proved the validity of these records. In the Samkhya philosophy, the Akashic records are recorded in the elements of akasha, elemental theory of Ancient India, called Mahabhuta.[3]

So, knowing this lineage and acceptance of the Akashic Records by ancient civilizations, but without the ability to venture into these realms ourselves, we are going to have to take a leap of faith in order to entertain Steiner's revelations.

Because I have had many supersensual experiences myself, some as clear to me and as real as this keyboard I am typing on, I can't discount the Akashic Records or Steiner's interpretations of these worlds. After many out-of-body experiences, visions in ayahuasca ceremonies, and visitations by both friendly and, as sometimes happens, some not-so-friendly immaterial entities, I know that there are other unseen forces and dimensions around us, so I can take that leap of faith and say that the Akashic Records seem to me just another aspect of reality.

Most of the time we can't see these worlds, which is fortunate, as it would be very hard to function on a day-to-day basis if we did. We are fortunate to have people like Steiner, Cayce, and Blavatsky who are comfortable navigating in both worlds to help relay these mysteries to us from the Akasha.

One thing we will discover is that all our psychic viewers of the Akashic Records claim that our Earth was populated with seed souls from other planets and star systems. Over time these soul entities— our ancestors according to these seers—mingled with and absorbed the etheric substance of the early forming Earth, and started to become more and more embodied. Originally, these beings were composed of a more misty or gaseous constitution due to the more gaseous and fiery Earth, but over eons of time their bodies would continue to evolve into what we can call a more humanoid form, especially with the densification of the planet. I would recommend reading Steiner's *Cosmic Memory* to learn more about this fascinating area about the cosmogony of humans.

In *Cosmic Memory* Steiner describes a very different constitution of an elite colony on the lost continent of Lemuria. He describes how this humanity had a more "plasticine" body that was more subject to internal soul qualities, as opposed to external forces, for its form. He said that this elite group had bodies that "changed form whenever the inner life changed," and were not subject to "the external influence of the region and climate." However, Steiner writes that even these soul-formed elites became subject to developing a more rigid body as it corresponded to "humanities evolutionary trajectory, but also with the densification of the planet."

Steiner says that it was only when man started to develop the faculty of reason, which corresponded with the densification of the world, and the hardening of rock, mineral, and metals, that human bodies began to become fairly unchanging.

Even though the earth was cooling down and all things were hardening, the ancient Lemurian climate was still an inhospitable place. Earthquakes and volcanic activity undermined the thin earth by continuous destructive activity, which created large and small streams of lava, and humans had to adapt to this fiery activity in everything they did. Steiner relates how they used "fire in their labors and contrivances" as modern peoples use artificial fire in their labors today.

Steiner's comment made me think of the monolithic Hanan Pacha type wakas and their unusual forms seemingly molded into the rock. Was the rock softened with fire to make these forms? And what about the evidence of vitrification? It does seem that someone knew how to weld and work with high heat with ease in the creation of these wakas. Even the caves below many of these wakas had evidence of some type of high temperature used in their construction.

I couldn't help but imagine what kinds of dwellings these early humans lived in if the world was hot and tumultuous. Surely, it was a mess above ground, but was it any better underground? According to Steiner it did seem that being underground was the better option for Lemurians:

The Lemurians did not have dwellings in our sense, except in their latest times. They lived where nature gave them the opportunity to do so. The caves, which they used, were only altered and extended insofar as necessary. Later they built such caves themselves and at that time they developed great skill for such constructions . . .

Steiner writes that early humans evolved and adapted with their environment, and because their physical constitution was less dense and ethereal at this time, the harsh environment was less of a concern, as they could adapt to the conditions more easily. One can imagine, however, that over the eons of time that Steiner relates the Lemurian period extended, that caves would be more important, as the body became more dense and physical and needed protection from the elements.

As far as evidence to support this cave-dwelling existence, one sees cave complexes all over the world, most notably in Peru, Syria, Turkey, Japan, and China, where tunnel systems are extensive. Is this where

Fig. 10.2. Cave entry at Sacsayhuaman.
See also Figures 5.1 and 5.2 on p. 78.

early humans sought shelter during particularly harsh episodes of geologic history? If the climate was inhospitable above ground, it certainly makes sense that more corporeal humans sought shelter down below it.

In spite of this inhospitable (or, at least, in our terms) environment, Lemurians did find time for creative endeavors. Steiner relates that the Lemurians created more "artful constructions" that "did not serve as dwellings." He continues:

> In the earliest times they originated in the desire to give to the things of nature a man-made form. Hills were remodeled in such a way that the form afforded man joy and pleasure. Stones were put together for the same purpose, or in order to be used for certain activities. The places where the children were hardened were surrounded with walls of this kind.
>
> Toward the end of this period, the buildings which served for the cultivation of "divine wisdom and divine art" and became more and more imposing and ornate. These institutions differed in every respect from what temples were later, for they were educational and scientific institutions at the same time.

One sees this kind of playfulness in form and function in both Hanan Pacha and Uran Pacha constructions, like the creators were using their powerful wills and imaginations to have fun with the rocks. Not only can one see the most lovely organic shapes, some flowing like undulating waves, and others suggesting organs of fertility, but one can also see very precise geometric shapes, including rectangle basins and platforms, circular and rectangular sillas, niches, and strange step-up chakana-like stairs. Usually, the organic and rectangular shapes are combined together in one masterful canvas of hardened limestone.

Were these monuments, like the ones seen at Sacsayhuaman and elsewhere around the world, also used as a type of scientific and educational learning institution that "served for the cultivation of this divine wisdom and divine art"? Here, Steiner goes more into detail about what the initiate was expected to master:

Fig. 10.3. Strange organic shapes at Little Q'enko.

He who was found fit was here initiated into the science of the universal laws and into the handling of them. If the Lemurian was a born magician, this talent was here developed into art and insight. Only those could be admitted who, through all kinds of discipline, had acquired the ability to overcome themselves to the greatest extent. For all others what went on in these institutions was the deepest secret. Here one learned to know and to control the forces of nature through direct contemplation of them. But the learning was such that in man the forces of nature changed into forces of the will. He himself could thereby execute what nature accomplishes.

If human will could control the forces of nature by direct contemplation is it possible that early humans could manipulate not only organic life, but the inorganic, just by using their force of will and imagination? This is a stunning thought and certainly brings to mind the idea of magic.

One of the distinctive features of Hanan Pacha monoliths is that one doesn't see the usual signs of typical tool cut marks. Instead, it seems as if someone brought a trowel and pressed it into the light grayish mass like it was putty. Occasionally, you will see what looks like fingerprints pushing up the material to form a water channel wall, grooves, or other features on the stone. In other places you see what looks like folded material that form sillas. If stone was softer in earlier times due to weaker gravity, and the people were dominated by a strong will that could penetrate the innermost forces of nature and work with it, perhaps this explains what we are seeing with these wakas.

Fig. 10.4. Monolith near the Moon Temple in Sacsayhuaman.

This powerful will is mentioned many times by Steiner as one of the distinguishing features that separated the elite Lemurians from later races. Steiner say that the Lemurian "derived the strength of his ideas from the objects which surrounded him" and absorbed the life force of growing plants and animals which helped him to understand their "inner action and life." This he could also do with lifeless objects as well. Without any engineering knowledge, the Lemurian knew where a stone would fit and where it would not, and what a tree could bear using "his faculty of imagination which acted with the sureness of a kind of instinct."

> Moreover, to a great extent, he had power over his own body. When it was necessary, he could increase the strength of his arm by a simple effort of the will. For example, he could lift enormous loads merely by using his will. If later the Atlantean was helped by his control of the life force, the Lemurian was helped by his mastery of the will. He was—the expression should not be misinterpreted—a born magician in all fields of lower human activities.

Could this will and strength of the Lemurians, along with their ability to lift enormous loads in a less densified world, explain how the massive stones seen at Sacsayhuaman or Ollantaytambo got there? I also think of the enigmatic Saywite Stone, which resides about forty-seven kilometers east of the city of Abancay, Peru. This large waka is approximately two meters wide by four meters long, and looks as if someone poured a liquid mass into some kind of pool, designed amazingly elaborate artwork on top, and then, after it hardened, moved it to its resting place on the Concacha hill. The stone is totally out of place in that natural environment, as there are no outcrops of this kind of stone in the area. Without a large crane—which there is no evidence the Inca had—it seems some kind of magical force moved this rock to its present site.

There are other wakas that also seem transported, including the Fractured Rock, which resides below the Saywite Stone, and the mysterious White Rock in Vilcabamba. Since so many of these wakas are massive, and unwieldy due to their irregular-shaped designs, it seems very unlikely that later cultures, like the Inca, brought them to their current resting places.

Were these massive stones lifted and transported by ancient Lemurians using the strength of their will and imagination, as well as

Fig. 10.5. The Saywite Stone near Abancay.

Fig. 10.6. Vilcabamba's White Rock.
Photo by AgainErick. See also color plate 15.

by their understanding the innermost life forces of the world around them? The writer and researcher Graham Hancock has commented that we should entertain this type of inquiry:

> At the Great Pyramid, at Baalbek, and at Sacsayhuaman, as well as at numerous other mysterious sites (such as the almost unbelievable Kailasa Temple, hewn out of solid basalt at Ellora in the Indian state of Maharashtra), intriguing ancient traditions persist. These traditions speak of meditating sages, the use of certain plants, the focused attention of initiates, miraculously speedy workmanship, and special kinds of chanting or tones played on musical instruments in connection with the lifting, placing, softening, and moulding of megaliths. My guess, confronted by the global distribution of such narratives and by the stark reality of the sites themselves, is that we're dealing with the reverberations of an ancient technology we don't understand, operating on principles that are utterly unknown to us.[5]

That is a pretty powerful comment by the man who has almost single-handedly changed the conversation about ancient humanity and civilization away from conventional models promoted by mainstream academia. However, it is comments like the above that get him dismissed and vilified by these same institutions. Hancock is committing the terrible sin of venturing into areas that no Western academic can verify with conventional science as it is known and practiced today. Until conventional science can penetrate into the worlds of the unseen, maybe by further explorations in quantum fields and psychic abilities, topics like these can only be categorized as speculation.

In the next section, we will explore other insights about early humanity by another famous esoteric, Madame Blavatsky.

## BLAVATSKY: A BRIDGE BETWEEN
## THE WEST AND THE EAST

It is hard to find a more mysterious and maligned individual than the philosopher and occultist Helena Petrovna Blavatsky (August 12, 1831–May 8, 1891). Founder of the influential and controversial Theosophy Movement—a religious and philosophical system based on a combination of Eastern beliefs and Western occultism—Blavatsky found herself frequently between two worlds very much at odds with one another: the more modern and materialistic West and the more esoteric and spiritual East. Frequently these two worlds collided in a spectacular fashion when forces came to attack her credibility and reputation based on her fantastic revelations.

However, at this time in history it was understandable that her writings would provoke shockwaves, as so much of what she was revealing was not only antithetical to the church, but to the new religion of materialistic science. She would be the punching bag for many who felt threatened by her psychic revelations, and accusations of fraud and charlatanism were to be part of her legacy.

Unlike Steiner, who was well educated and had a mind accustomed to the scientific workings and methodologies of the twentieth century, Blavatsky was self-educated and more accustomed to living in the rarified air of psychic worlds and spiritualism, so it was easier to attack her for what were considered her supernatural and, to many critics, her unscientific beliefs. However, like Steiner, she was an untiring workhorse when it came to relaying estoteric wisdom, revealed to her by masters, to others. She wrote several major works, including the influential *Isis Unveiled* and *The Secret Doctrine*, written in 1875 and 1888 respectively, both of which are occult classics today.

*The Secret Doctrine* is Blavatsky's most important book, and the first volume, *Cosmogenesis*, is an exposition on the composition and evolution of the universe based on seven stanzas from the secret *Book of Dzyan*, with commentary and explanations from Blavatsky. The second

Fig. 10.7. Helena Petrovna Blavatsky.

volume, *Anthropogenesis*, contains another series of stanzas from the *Book of Dzyan*, describing the processes of human evolution.

Blavatsky, is said to have been introduced to this lore when she was studying estoteric texts in Tibet. She claimed that the book, written in the sacred language of Senzar, had been historically safeguarded from profane eyes by initiates of an Occult Brotherhood. Blavatsky claimed she could penetrate the obscure language with the help of Tibetan masters, the mahatmas, who allowed her to read the book.

It is claimed that Madame Blavatsky wrote both *Isis Unveiled* and *The Secret Doctrine* with the help of these mahatmas, or spiritual teachers, and that they sometimes transferred their consciousness to her physical body in a process called *tulku*. Blavatsky said that these mahatmas were real human beings in physical bodies and not spirits, in all likelihood to avoid provoking the ire of the church who were against mediumship. According to her, these teachers instructed her through the astral light and at other times, while she slept. She said entire pages were generated by them through her own handwriting.

Because of these visions and interactions with the mahatmas, Blavatsky was the first person from the West to explain the Eastern esoteric concepts that have never been clearly given out to the public before, including those about the nature of the cosmos, and the origins and nature of humanity. It was from her books that the seven root races and the seven sub-races of mankind were expounded.

Like Steiner, Blavatsky said that early human races were of a much more ethereal nature, and over an immense period of time evolved into a denser form:

> Man's organism was adapted in every race to its surroundings. The first Root-Race was as ethereal as ours is material. The progeny of the seven Creators, who evolved the seven primordial Adams, surely required no purified gases to breathe and live upon . . . Therefore, however strongly the impossibility of this teaching may be urged by the devotees of modern science, the Occultist maintains that the case was as stated *æons of years* before even the evolution of the Lemurian, the first physical man, which itself took place 18,000,000 years ago.[6]

I would encourage anybody interested in learning more about the seven root races to visit the Theosophy World Resource Center website for a short exposition about this fascinating subject, but, in order to not get too sidetracked from the focus of this book—Hanan and Uran Pacha and their possible builders—let's see if Blavatsky says anything that can shine light on this matter. Fortunately she does. In a section called "Cyclopean Ruins and Colossal Stones as Witnesses to Giants," she writes about the circular stones found in the British Isles:

Irish tradition attributes the origin of her circular stones to a *Sorcerer who brought them from Africa*. De Mirville sees in that sorcerer "an accursed *Hamite*." We see in him a dark Atlantean, or perhaps even some earlier Lemurian, who had survived till the birth of the British Islands—Giants in every and any case.[7]

Because Blavatsky was British and spent a great deal of time in Tibet and India, it doesn't surprise me that she doesn't say too much about the rock monoliths and megaliths in South America; however, she does mention the gigantic statues found in Easter Island:

> The Easter Island relics are, for instance, the most astounding and eloquent memorials of the primeval giants. They are as grand as they are mysterious; and one has but to examine the heads of the colossal statues, that have remained unbroken on that island, to recognize in them at a glance the features of the type and character attributed to the Fourth Race giants. They seem of one cast though different in features—that of a *distinctly sensual type*, such as the Atlanteans (the Daityas and "Atalantians") are represented to have in the esoteric Hindu books.[8]

. . . and, she connects them to Peru by quoting an extract from Robert Brown's book *The Countries of the World*, in Vol. IV, page 43:

> . . . we find the Lemurians in their sixth sub-race building their first rock-cities out of stone and lava. One of such great cities of primitive structure was built entirely of lava, some thirty miles west from where Easter Island now stretches its narrow piece of sterile ground, and was entirely destroyed by a series of volcanic eruptions. The oldest remains of Cyclopean buildings were all the handiwork of the Lemurians of the last sub-races; and an occultist shows, therefore, no wonder on learning that the stone relics found on the small piece of land called Easter Island by Captain Cook, are "very much like

the walls of the Temple of Pachacamac or the Ruins of Tia-Huanuco in Peru."

Blavatsky definitely saw a race of giants as the crafters of these massive stone monuments, and I had to wonder if she was indeed correct, as I have seen many structures in Peru that also look as if designed for Giants. For instance, one can find on the grounds leading up to the Grand Chincana (a giant waka located north of the citadel walls of Sacsayhuaman) steps so big one has to climb up, on hands and knees, from the first step to the second step. And, then, when one gets to the monument itself, the visitor sees thrones way too large for the average human body. Equally as intriguing is that around and on top of these large thrones, one sometimes sees very small seats, as if made for children, as if the giants made seats for their offspring or perhaps smaller beings they worked with.

Blavatsky also mentions in *The Secret Doctrine* that some stones and stone monuments had the ability to "speak" and "take flight" as well as "dance." She writes, "It is also known that the famous stone at Westminster was called *liafail*—'the speaking stone,'—which raised its voice only to name the king that had to be chosen" and "Suidas speaks of a certain Heraclius, who could distinguish at a glance the inanimate stones from those which were endowed with motion; and Pliny mentions stones which 'ran away when a hand approached them.'"

Blavatsky gives an example from Apollonius Rhodius who "expatiates on the rocking stones, and says that they are 'stones placed on the apex of a tumulus, and so sensitive *as to be movable by the mind*' (*Ackerman's Arth. Index*, p. 34), referring no doubt to the ancient priests who moved such stones by will-power and from a distance."

As far as the stones speaking, she doesn't give any firsthand accounts, but her passages remind me of a story I read in Freddy Silva's book *The Divine Blueprint*, were he recalls the download he got from a standing stone in Wales. He writes of reaching out to touch the stone "whereupon a magnetic force" pulled his hand to its surface and "all the while marriages, births, ceremonies, duels, festivities, deaths and whole cycles of lives and gossip were downloaded into my head."[8]

Silva's story brings up some thoughts I have about these stones. We do know that the ancients carefully chose their stones to carry out various functions, and, they went to great pains, and, sometimes, great distances, to get just the right stones for their purposes. Most stones used in temples and menhirs (standing stones) are made of a high-quartz content granite, which not only gives off a electrostatic charge but amplifies sound. Some of this granite contains very high amounts of magnetite, a similar composition to the menhirs at Carnak, such that these create a "magnetic field."

Also, most of these sites sit on water sources and, today, German scientists have discovered that water holds memory[9] and believe as water travels, so does the information stored in it. If we add in the amplifying and storage capabilities of quartz, as well as the magnetic fields and telluric currents that are concentrated around these sites, one wonders if these monuments are not actual recording and communication devices. Is this why Silva got such a vivid download when he touched the rock in Wales?

Blavatsky equally implies that these stones were for communication and "magic," and writes:

The hugest of them are evidently the relics of the Atlanteans; the smaller ones, such as Brinham Rocks, with some revolving stones on their summit, are copies from the more ancient lithoi . . . As it is, we know that they were universally used during long prehistoric ages, and all for the same purposes of prophecy and magic.[10]

Today, most archaeologists speculate that megaliths and monoliths are designed solely for tracking celestial objects and for marking the equinoxes and solstices, but they seem unaware of the inherent magical properties of the stone itself and the telluric currents in our environment.

If the stone can "speak," "take flight," and "dance," shouldn't we be tuning in to what they have to say?

Before we end this section, we will look at one more mystic's view into the Akashic Records for his insights into early humanity.

## A HINDU MYSTIC'S VISION

Here I would like to introduce a more contemporary reader into the Akashic Records, one Sivaya Subramuniya, who wrote a book about his revelations titled *Lemurian Scrolls*. But, first, a little background about Subramuniya is needed. From the website of Kauai's Hindu Monastery:

> In 1947, as a young man of 20, he journeyed to India and Sri Lanka and two years later was initiated into sannyasa by the renowned siddha yogi and worshiper of Siva, Jnanaguru Yogaswami (1872–1964) of Sri Lanka, regarded as one of the 20th century's most remarkable mystics.
>
> For over five decades Subramuniya, affectionately known as Gurudeva, taught Hinduism to Hindus and seekers from all faiths. In the line of successorship, he was the 162nd Jagadacharya of the Nandinatha Sampradaya's Kailasa Parampara and Guru Mahasannidhanam of Kauai Aadheenam (also known as Kauai's Hindu Monastery), a 382-acre temple-monastery complex on Hawaii's Garden Island.[11]

The Hindu and Indian culture scholar Klaus Klostermaier once described Subramuniya as "the single-most advocate of Hinduism outside India."[12]

In *Lemurian Scrolls*, Subramuniya, like Steiner and Blavatsky, read the Akasha, and too explained how humans originally came from the stars and how a fire planet was essential for his development. In the first chapter, "Pilgrimage to Planet Earth," we read:

The Need For a Fire Planet:

Mankind migrated to this planet in his divine soul body during the Sat Yuga, the age of enlightenment. He had reached a final stage of evolution on his native planet. The risk in migrating to a fire planet was great, but so was the reward. They were, however, at a place in evolution requiring a planet with fire in it to catalyze them through new experiences into completing their unfoldment to the final realization of the Self. Souls came from the other planets to Earth for one of two reasons: either they came to realize the Self, because they had not previously done so and were just drifting in bliss, or were great beings who already had the Self realized and came to help the others. They came from everything in a state of status quo. They had come to this planet to get jostled around in the fire to continue their unfoldment.

And, like Steiner and Gamarra, Subramuniya mentions that the fauna and flora of this era were huge. He writes, "We are told that at the end of the Tretâ Yuga all life on this planet—humans, animals, trees, plants, flowers—was twice the size that they are now. It has changed so much, and it is predicted that by the end of the Kali Yuga all will be half again as small."[13]

■ ■ ■

In the next chapter we will explore the issue of time and how it is seen from the views of our Akashic readers.

# 11

# Time:
# Relatively Speaking

*Why is it so difficult for us to think in relative terms?
Well, for the good reason that human nature loves
absoluteness, and erroneously considers it as a state of
higher knowledge.*

FELIX ALBA-JUEZ, "WHO WAS RIGHT:
PTOLEMY OR COPERNICUS?"

One thing that has presented a problem for me in this book is the assigning of dates from the recordings of the Akashic investigators to epochs in the far past. It just so happens that we get wildly different timelines from all of them. For instance, Blavatsky is quoted as saying in *The Secret Doctrine, Vol. 2* that the first truly physical human appeared sometime around eighteen million years ago, during the cusp of the early Atlantean period,[1] while Subramuniya says it was around four million years ago, and that this early human was Lemurian.[2] Cayce says there was one early type of primitive humanity on Earth ten and a half million years ago.[3] Steiner is a bit more vague on time—I think wisely so—and says the duration of the Lemurian period took place over an immensely long time and saw the transition of humans from non-corporeal beings to physical ones.[4] What is going on with the widely divergent theories about time from our Akashic readers?

Our confusion about the vague timelines poses a big problem for those of us who like concrete things to chew on—like yummy dates—when studying historical events. Accuracy also helps give us a compass to follow as to whether the researchers involved are deemed "credible." However, we should take to heart the message the late Sandy Denny imparts in her song "Who Knows Where the Times Goes?"—especially this stanza:

> *Sad, deserted shore, your fickle friends are leaving*
> *Ah, but then you know, it's time for them to go.*
> *But I will still be here, I have no thought of leaving*
> *I do not count the time.*

Yes, my fickle friends will probably find issues with the wildly varying timelines from the psychic investigators. But before you leave, just know this obfuscation in timelines may be entirely due to the very nature of the Akasha, as well as the particular education of our investigators, as the Akasha is a place where the records of all humanity—past, future, and present—are stored, without a convenient chronological chart to go with it. For those that may not be familiar with the Akasha, it is a metaphysical library that contains everything a soul has experienced from the moment it was created, and time does not exist there. In the physical plane, we see time in a linear sense; in the Akashic Records, everything exists at the same time.

So it turns out that the Akashic readers can only make educated guesses at the particular time these events in history took place, based on what they see in their visions and what they know about geological time, especially ancient geological time. This is not an easy endeavor at all, as I can attest, even with the aid of modern tools like Google.

However, there may be a solution to the sticky date issue. For example, if we can analyze what is said by the Akashic readers about the environment they see, maybe we can find clues as to what time in Earth's geological history we are talking about. Let's start with Rudolf Steiner.

In *Cosmic Memory*, Steiner writes about the fauna and flora of the Lemurian times. He writes that the atmosphere was "much thicker" than in later Atlantean times, and that the water was "thinner." He says that the crust of the earth "was not yet as hard as it would become later," and that of animal life, only birds, amphibians and lower mammals had developed. The modern higher mammals did not yet exist. The flora resembled "our palms and similar trees" and had formed in "mighty forests." And, that all forms were of "gigantic sizes."[5]

Regarding his comments on the fauna of the times, Steiner doesn't mention any dinosaurs in this description, and he says that higher mammals didn't exist. Unfortunately, he doesn't give a clue as to what the mammals looked like, so maybe we can assume they were the shrew-like or proto-simian ancestors to our present-day mammal orders.

Subramuniya, like Steiner, mentions that early Earth in the Lemurian age the "air was thick and the Earth lush and tropical" with "thick clouds of gasses and healthful substances floating in the air," and that these "healthful" substances were used eventually to materialize a body around the soul's etheric body. Subramuniya also writes that the "fauna and flora were huge" being "twice the size they are now." In his description he includes humans as well.[6]

It was a bit harder pinning down a good description of the early Lemurian period climate from Madame Blavatsky, but in her classic, *The Secret Doctrine, Vol. 2* in the chapter titled the "Evolution of the Sweat Born" (an evolutionary stage of the early Lemurians), she refers to a time that scientists of her day said was filled with "deadly gases, and of elements entirely saturated with carbon and nitrogen, in which the vegetable and animal kingdoms are shown to have lived, thriven, and developed."[7]

Blavatsky believes that it was a misnomer to describe this atmosphere as "deadly" because the humans at that time were of a more etheric nature and had not yet developed bodies where the increased nitrogen and carbon in the atmosphere could harm them.

Blavatsky, additionally, mentions that during the "second portion" of the Lemurian race that the Earth was semitropical and "most adapted to the primitive wants of nascent physical man."[8] And, in the later Lemurian period, a period that Blavatsky says was the period of the Giants, we read that this was when they had started to make their first buildings of stone and lava,[9] so we assume that the era was still volcanic in nature.

So, it seems that the ancient Lemurian, in all his forms—from etheric to more solid states—lived in a climate that was lush, hot, and volcanic.

## HOT PLANET, LARGE FLORA
## AND FAUNA: WHERE IN TIME ARE WE?

It has taken me a while to isolate a particular time in Earth's geologic history that might fit the descriptions seen by our Akashic viewers. The problem is that there have been many times where the Earth had megathermal events, hot enough to be called a "fire planet," so I had to look for clues about what was said about the flora and fauna that matched our readers' descriptions.

There are two geological periods that possibly fit the descriptions of the Earth seen by our Akashic viewers: the Eocene and Miocene periods. These periods show substantial periods of warmth, massive forestation, larger animals, and very active volcanism. However, it seems to me that the Eocene period (56 to 33.9 million years ago)[10] more closely matches the world as described by our viewers, as the Miocene (23 to 5.33 million years ago), has a fossil record of higher order modern mammals and is known of a period of extensive grasslands, not tropical forests.[11]

Blavatsky gives a date of 18 million years for the creation of the first physical man, which would put these "Titans" in the geological timeframe of the Miocene. However, possibly the vast time that transpired in the evolution of humanity may have seen the Lemurians of a more plasticine nature come into existence in the Eocene and become more solid during the Miocene as Blavatsky suggests. Here she argues against the prevailing modern scientific view of her day (and ours) that man could not have existed in those hoary Eocene times:

> . . . it is quite certain that no terrestrial conditions whatever negative the hypothesis of an Eocene Man, if evidence for his reality is forthcoming. Occultists, who maintain that the above date carries us far back into the secondary or "Reptilian" age, may refer to M. de Quatrefages in support of the possible existence of man in that remote antiquity. But with regard to the earliest Root-Races the case is very different. If the thick agglomeration of vapours, charged with carbonic acid, that escaped from the soil or was held in suspension in the atmosphere since the commencement of sedimentation, offered a fatal obstacle to the life of human organisms as now known, how, it will be asked, could the primeval men have existed? This consideration is, in reality, out of court. Such terrestrial conditions as were then operative had no touch with the plane on which the evolution of the *ethereal astral* races proceeded. Only in relatively recent geological periods, has the spiral course of cyclic law swept mankind into the lowest grade of physical evolution—the plane of gross material causation. In those early ages, *astral* evolution was alone in progress, and the two planes, the astral and the physical, though developing on parallel lines, had no direct point of contact with one another.[12]

If the Eocene was the beginning stages of the Lemurian epoch, it would explain the hot "fire planet" that our Akashic viewers describe. What we do know about this period is that it starts with a very unusual heating event called Paleocene–Eocene Thermal Maximum (PETM). This period was marked with a rapid release of greenhouse gasses, which many scientists believe was due to volcanism and the release of carbon and methane from the ocean floor associated with the North Atlantic Igneous Province. Fossil records show that at the PETM the Earth's average temperature was about five to eight degrees Celcius higher than today, though some estimates are even higher.[13]

We do know that the Eocene was a time when carbon dioxide and oxygen levels were much higher: carbon dioxide levels reached 1,000 parts per million in the Early Eocene, more than twice the present-day level of 412 ppm,"[14] and oxygen levels to twice as much too.[15] Since, carbon and oxygen are the building blocks of life, it seems like this period could have been the epoch where our early ancestors built their bodies as they densified.

This epoch seems to be a matching period for a "fiery planet" with "thick clouds of gasses" as the viewers describe. Let's examine the fauna and flora to see what other clues we can hone in on to discover our timeframe for the first Lemurians.

## *Fauna*

The Early Eocene saw a die-off of many marine life forms including the single-cell organism benthic foraminifera, and saw the massive increase in acidification of the oceans from the PETM event mentioned earlier. However, on land, other life forms were expanding and thriving including the first ancestors of the modern mammal orders (including primates), which suddenly appeared in Europe and in North America.

This period also marked the appearance of two new groups of animals: the perissodactyls, which were the ancestors to our modern-day horses, rhinoceroses, and tapirs; and the artiodactyls, ancestors to our modern day deer, cattle, and sheep. This was also a time where whales transitioned from terrestrial to fully aquatic animals and bird diversification expanded greatly. Also, reptiles were abundant during this time. In the early Eocene dwarfism was common in many mammals. It was thought that smaller bodies could better tolerate the heat of that period; however, over time with the cooling of the planet during the

Middle and Late Eocene, when mammals left the forest for the grass-lands many of them became noticeably larger. At this time we begin to see megafauna like the *Uintatherium*, *Arsinoitherium*, and brontotheres, mammals that look a lot like today's rhinoceroses and hippopotamuses, and large bear-dog-like predators called Hyaenodon and Daphoenus.[17]

## *Flora*

During the early–middle Eocene, the Earth became ice-free and lush tropical and paratropical forests covered most of the planet. Even the polar regions had quite extensive forests. Scientists have discovered fossils of swamp cypress and dawn redwood on Ellsmere Island in the Arctic, and palm trees in Alaska and Northern Europe. In the end of the late period, as the earth cooled, more deciduous trees began to take over in large parts of North America and Eurasia.[18]

## NOT LEAVING A MARK

Though it seems impossible for early humans to be living so long ago in our geologic past, especially if you look at it from the perspective of Western orthodox beliefs, if we look at humanity in a more esoteric sense—as spiritual beings evolving and becoming more densified over time, like so many ancient spiritual traditions declare—then maybe it is possible to envision incorporeal humans existing over fifty million years ago. Also, if these ancestors did evolve from a nonphysical, etheric state to a more physical one over time, it could explain why no human remains have been found from the time of the Eocene fossil record. William Q. Judge, one of the founders of the original Theosophical Society, explains this theory:

> At the time of the huge antediluvian animals they absorbed in their enormous bodies so much of the total quantity of gross matter available for frames of sentient beings that the astral man remained without a corporeal frame, as yet unclothed "with coats of skin." For this

reason he could exist in the same place with those huge birds and reptiles without fear. Their massive proportions inspired him with no terror, and by their consumption of food there was no lessening of his sustenance. And, therefore, being of such a composition that he left no impression upon mud or plastic rock, the death of one astral body after another left no fossil and no mark to be unearthed by us in company with the very beasts and birds which were his contemporaries. . . . his remains could not be deposited in any stratum until such time as he had grown to sufficient hardness. . . . While, therefore, our explorers are finding, now and then, the remains of animals and birds and reptiles in strata which show an age far greater than any assigned to the human race, they never come upon human skeletons. How could man leave any trace at a stage when he could not press himself into the clay or be caught by soft lava or masses of volcanic dust?[19]

This brings up another question: If early humanity could not leave a footprint in "mud or plastic rock," how did they leave their marks in Hanan Pacha or Uran Pacha monoliths? Well, I presume we are looking at a time when humans had enough density to do so, sometime in the later Lemurian period.

## LEAVING THEIR MARK

Blavatsky pinpoints the time when the first physical humans came into existence around 18 million years ago, and that this was a time that the Lemurians built many of their first Cyclopean buildings* from stone and lava, implying that the times were fiery and that they could master those elements with relative ease:

---

*Cyclopean comes from the Greek word for "Cyclops", a race of giants that left their mark using large irregular-shaped rocks without mortar.

Yet, we find the Lemurians in their sixth subrace building their first rock-cities out of stone and lava. One of such great cities of primitive structure was built entirely of lava, some thirty miles west from where Easter Island now stretches its narrow piece of sterile ground, and was entirely destroyed by a series of volcanic eruptions. The oldest remains of Cyclopean buildings were all the handiwork of the Lemurians of the last sub-races; and an occultist shows, therefore, no wonder on learning that the stone relics found on the small piece of land called Easter Island by Captain Cook, are "very much like the walls of the Temple of Pachacamac or the Ruins of Tia-Huanuco [Tiwanaku] in Peru," ("The Countries of the World," by Robert Brown, Vol. 4, p. 43); and that they are in the Cyclopean style.[20]

I hope this last sentence by Blavatsky does not escape the attention of the reader as it could pinpoint a timeframe, and an origin, for the makers of polygonal megalithic sites. However, unfortunately, I have not been able to find a mention of any Hanan Pacha–style monoliths in *The Secret Doctrine*.

## CONFOUNDING TIME

Though pinpointing a date like Blavatsky does with the builders of the megalithic sites is helpful, assigning this to a geological epoch is a challenge as geological periods keep expanding and contracting, even in mainstream science. For instance, it is claimed by Theosophists that Lemuria existed around 34 million years ago,[21] and that the first human was prior to the pre-Tertiary period. In *The Secret Doctrine, Vol. 2* she writes:

The claim that physical man was originally a colossal pre-tertiary giant, and that he existed 18,000,000 years ago, must of course appear preposterous to admirers of, and believers in, modern learning. The whole posse comitatis of biologists will turn away from the conception of this third race Titan of the Secondary age, a being fit to fight as successfully with the then gigantic monsters of the air, sea, and land.[22]

The Tertiary Period is a term that describes a geologic period from 66 million to 2.6 million years ago, although today it no longer used to delineate geological time.[23] Is Blavatsky implying that there was a human being who was around at the time of the Jurassic, which would be "pre-Tertiary"? Or someone who lived just before the Cretaceous–Paleogene extinction event, the event that destroyed the dinosaurs?

We can see here that we have a problem. If this giant was supposed to be pre-Tertiary, he can't be eighteen million years old! Once again the timelines are significantly off. However, and I must state this mantra again—*time is relative*. When *The Secret Doctrine* was written in 1888, geological time was much more condensed and confusing, and the dating tools that we use today to examine rock and ice were not created yet. In fact, Blavatsky says this about the confusion of the timelines:

> Sir Charles Lyell, who is credited with having "happily invented the terms Eocene, Miocene, and Pliocene," to mark the three divisions of the Tertiary age, ought really to have settled upon some approximate age for his "Mind-offspring." Having left the duration of these periods, however, to the speculations of specialists, the greatest confusion and perplexity are the result of that happy thought. It seems like a hopeless task to quote one set of figures from one work, without the risk of finding it contradicted by the same Author in an earlier or a subsequent volume.[24]

*Bingo!* An astute observation by Blavatsky for sure. Unfortunately, in Blavatsky's era geologists really had no idea how old the sun, Earth, and cosmos were, and she gives various examples. For instance, she relates how eminent geologist Sir W. Thomson changed his opinion about the ages of Earth and the Sun "about half-a-dozen times," and that he believed the Earth "allows 60 millions of years since the beginning of the Cambrian period," and in Thomson and Tait's *Natural Philosophy* she writes that "one finds only ten million years allow, since the time when the temperature of the Earth permitted vegetable life to appear on it."[25]

Today scientists concur that the Cambrian period was 539–485 million years in the past,[26] so even the exact knowledge Blavatsky was looking for in the late nineteenth century to align esoteric doctrine with scientific dogma is significantly off from markers of geologic time as we know it today. It is unclear if this Lemurian Titan that she wrote about was really living around eighteen million years ago as she could be referencing an earlier time—or to a later time, for that matter.

Subramuniya also had questions as to how to mark time, especially in light of the fact that we are talking about incredibly vast timeframes. Since the modern interpretation of a year is marked by how many days our Earth takes to orbit the sun, this proves a problem for accurate dating if the Earth orbit has been constantly changing. Subramuniya, like Gamarra, says in his book, *Lemurian Scrolls*, that the Earth's orbit was doing exactly this:

> We must keep in mind that a "year" is a period that can also vary in these vast timeframes, as the Earth's orbit around the sun has been constantly changing since the Earth came into being.[27]

Subramuniya also points out that Hindu calculations of time are based on four yugas—Sat, Tretâ, Dvâpara, and Kali Yuga—which are approximately 432,000 years apiece, and which repeat an additional four more times according to the cosmology of Sanâtana Dharma, lasting a total of 4,320,000 years.[28]

This is just a smaller cycle within a much greater cycle in time called the *manvantara*, an enormous period lasting 308,478,000 years, based on the approximate time it takes for the Earth and our solar system to revolve around the galaxy.[29] It truly is a remarkable, but complex, system of marking time.

In the 2006 second edition of Subraminiya's *Lemurian Scrolls*, the editors say that they adjusted Subraminiya's original time references to reflect the expanded manvantara as it aligns more closely with events corroborated by Western science.[30]

> Each manvantara consists of 71 *chaturyugas*. . . . Here, by interpreting "cycle of yugas" as manvantara, the statement concurs with the discoveries of modern archaeology. Science states that the first plant and animal life appeared on Earth during this second manvantara, which began approximately 61 million years ago. A manvantara, from the Sanskit Manu and antara, meaning, "an age of a Manu (or man)," roughly corresponds to the length of time it takes our solar system to make a complete revolution around the Central Sun, or galactic center.[31]

Though this addition to the book is an improvement over the past measurement of time recorded in the first edition, I am still a bit stumped as modern science says plant and animal life started much further back, with cyanobacteria pumping out oxygen as early as 2.1 billion years ago and multicellular animals coming into being about 800 million years ago.[32]

## OLDER STILL

If we want to entertain a more extreme timeline, one where the Earth was 55 percent smaller—as Alfredo Gamarra's Three Worlds Cosmogony postulates—that would be in two-hundred-million-year-old range, and that could conceivably work with the descriptions of the Akashic readers. We would be in the Triassic Period, when the first true mammals—the therapsids—were said to evolve. It was an age dominated by amphibians, reptiles and birds, and large fern forests. The dinosaurs had not yet taken center stage (although their ancestors were around) until sometime after the Triassic–Jurassic extinction event at the end of this period. During this time the Earth saw huge volcanic eruptions that occurred as the supercontinent Pangaea began to break apart, forming the Central Atlantic Magmatic Province.[33]

This timeframe also could explain the hypothesis of the expanding Earth and explain a time of less gravity, which according to Gamarra and some of our Akashic viewers helped early man manipulate matter using his superior will and imagination.

## A WORD ON ATLANTIS

Before we end this chapter, I think it would be a good idea to mention something about Atlantis. I didn't spend as much time on this topic because I never felt that Hanan Pacha constructions were Atlantean, and, it seems, according to Blavatsky, neither were the Uran Pacha megalithic constructions. It is my assumption that the fourth race constructed the grand and precise pyramids that we see around the world. Blavatsky even suggests these are Atlantean artifacts as well:

> The Pyramids are closely connected with the ideas of both the Great Dragon (the constellation), the "Dragons of Wisdom," or the great Initiates of the Third and Fourth Races, and the Floods of the Nile, regarded as a divine reminder of the great Atlantic Flood. The astronomical records of Universal History, however, are said to have had their beginnings with the Third Sub-race of the Fourth Root-race or the Atlanteans.[34]

As fascinating as the subject of Atlantis is, there has been so much written on the subject that I decided not to expand on this topic in great depth. However, I would like to say that there are some similarities in the megalithic styles seen in Peru with those seen on the Egyptian pyramids, including stones with pronounced knob features and megalithic polygonal stone walls that look like they were created with geopolymers. Blavatsky does say that Lemuria and its later people were the first megalith builders, and this island nation came before Atlantis; however, there was some overlap between the two civilizations. She writes: "It *did* exist [Atlantis] most assuredly, as it was fast approaching its greatest days of glory and civilization when the last of the Lemurian continents went down."[35] and the elite Lemurian race gave birth to the fourth Atlantean race.[36] This may account for some of the similarities that we can see in their construction methods but differences in the buildings styles.

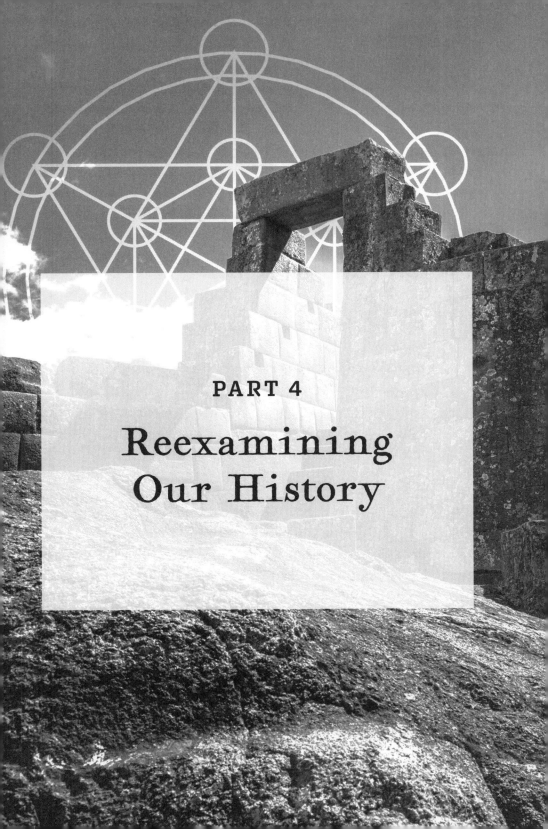

PART 4

# Reexamining
# Our History

# 12

# Stone Oddities

*We need . . . to keep enchantment alive in our descriptions of nature:*
*to provide celebrations of not quite knowing, of wonder, of mystification.*

ROBERT MACFARLANE

## THE MYSTERIOUS "PUMA PAW"

One of the things I like about Cusco's old town is that almost everywhere one turns one finds something weird and remarkable, and the Limacpampa Chico square area is no exception. Standing high on a fountain pedestal in the plaza is a strange rock with what looks to be a rather large footprint of, all I can say is—something. The locals say it is a puma paw print, but it looks like no puma print I know of. The puma prints I have seen have always had four digits and a pad, but in this print there is a fifth digit that is separated from the four main digits and is articulated off to the side, slightly laterally, like a thumb. Also, with a puma print you would see some kind of claw depression, and here there are none. And, this print is huge—maybe one and a half meters in length! If this were a puma it would have had to be about forty feet long!

Fig. 12.1. The "Puma Paw," Limacpampa Chico Square. Cusco.

Another weird aspect of the rock is that it looks like it has Hanan Pacha forms pressed into it, both in the back and on top. What exactly is going on here? Was there some kind of animal living during the

Hanan Pacha time that created this print, and were they around with humans at the same time when the stone was soft?

My mind started reeling with the possibilities, including the idea that this may not be an actual footprint of an animal at all, but a facsimile of one made by the creators of the forms that lie above and around it. I cannot at this point rule this out, but if it is a real animal footprint, then what kind of animal could have created it? I decided to research what kinds of animals had five digits on their feet, and to see if we could pinpoint a time when this animal, if real, existed.

What I discovered is that bears and their cousins, the raccoons, have five digits, but they usually have very pronounced claws, and these claws almost always leave some kind of imprint, along with their digits and pads in footprints. This is something that the Cusco print lacks, as I see no evidence of claw marks. It also seemed very doubtful that any of the relatives of bears or raccoons could have left a print so large, although we know that there were giant bears in South America around two hundred thousand years ago—approximately twice the size of a modern grizzly bear, but not large enough to make a print this size.

I did find something very intriguing in my research: there were dinosaurs in the past called sauropods, which did have five toes, and would be large enough to make a footprint this size.

Sauropods are known as being some of the largest dinosaurs that walked the Earth, and for decades scientists believed that these creatures had to be semi-aquatic due to their massive size not being able to sustain their heavy weight on land—a belief that today is now rejected. Sauropods also had ridiculously long necks and frequently tails of a similar length. They evolved into many different shapes and sizes during a long period on Earth, from about 200 million years ago to 65 million years ago, at which time the Permian Collapse occurred, and killed off most of the large dinosaurs. Sauropods did live in South America, and one of the largest ones ever found was in Argentina, appropriately called Argentinosaurus.

Most of the examples I found with a Google image search of sauropod footprints were of such poor quality that it was hard to make out the finer foot details, but I eventually found some drawings from the Cleveland Museum of Natural History that gave nice outlines of the various prints of sauropod feet. What I could make out is that the prints were usually in a fairly round shape—like a tree trunk—and there was some kind of evidence of digits that pressed out laterally along the sides.

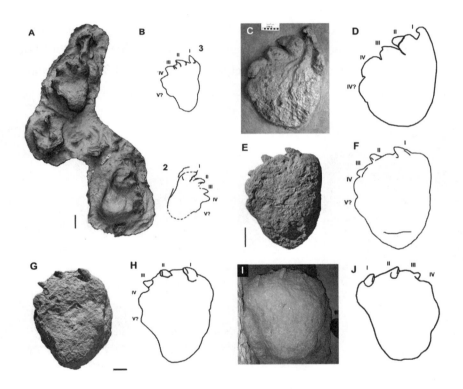

Fig. 12.2. Sauropod hind feet.
Photo from Cleveland Museum of Natural History.

However, these prints seem to be representations of the hind feet, according to paleontologists at the Cleveland Museum of Natural History and Dickinson Museum Center (North Dakota):

"Sauropod hind-feet possess enlarged, flattened claws which folded across and under the foot when the animal squeezed or 'flexed' its foot muscles," said lead author Lee Hall, Vertebrate Paleontology Preparator at The Cleveland Museum of Natural History. "When foot muscles are flexed in a human, the toes are pulled straight down. When a sauropod flexed its toes the claws folded across the front of the foot, rotating downwards, creating an overlapping stack of flat scrapers."[1]

Obviously, the hind feet of a sauropod do not match the "Puma Paw" print, but what about the front feet? It seems that there could be a match here with the Opisthocoelicaudia (see fig. 12.3 below, image

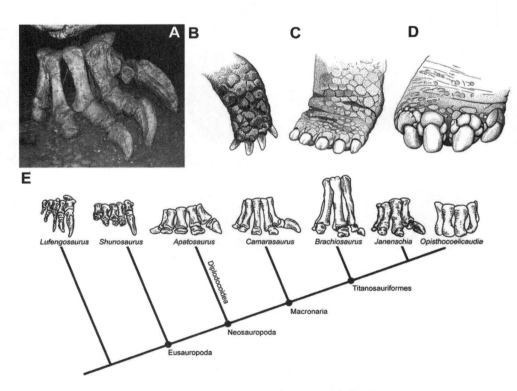

Fig. 12.3. Types of sauropod feet.
Photo from Cleveland Museum of Natural History.

to the far right), although it doesn't look like they ever found a foot-print in such excellent shape as the "Puma Paw" print to make a good comparison.

If this were an actual sauropod print, it would have had to have been made at least sixty-five million years ago, and because there is tell-tale Hanan Pacha work on top and around it, would this imply that there was some early type of human that was around at the time that the print was made? Of course, we don't know if the Hanan Pacha work came later on this stone, or indeed if the print was created by the same individual(s) who also put in the more abstract angled shapes on the top and the back of the stone.

Whatever the source, I would love to see an archaeologist or ich-nologist take a good look at it—if for no other reason than to disprove this crazy theory.

## THE ICA STONES

In the village of Ica in Peru, there is a small private museum created by Peruvian physician Dr. Javier Cabrera that displays what are now known as the Ica Stones. Many of these strange stones show humans co-mingling with dinosaur-like creatures, carrying out advanced sur-gery and stargazing through telescopes, as well as depictions of humans doing more mundane activities, like fishing, pottery-making, and hav-ing sex. Although most scholars have dismissed these stones as frauds—and, admittedly there are people doing crude knock-offs of them to sell as souvenirs to tourists—others are deemed authentic, as they were excavated by archaeologists, in situ, in century-old tombs, and today are housed in government museums. The ones collected by Cabrera in his private museum also show unmistakable patinas, along with the typical film of oxidation on them, that couldn't have been simulated in modern times, according to David Woetzel and Dennis Swift.

These researchers did an independent blind test on three stones: one of unknown provenance coming from the Cabrera Museum, one found by archaeologists and accepted as an authentic artifact now in the Rio Grand Palpa Museum, and one recently made in an Ica souvenir shop.

They sent the samples to Mason Optical, Inc. of Hillsboro, Oregon, to be analyzed using their jumbo stereoscopic microscope. When the results came back it was established that the souvenir shop stone was a recent production because of a lack of a natural patina and angled incisions; however, the Cabrera stone, "revealed a fine patina, embedded dirt, and natural oxidations, solid evidence of [age] authenticity" and that both the Cabrera and the Rio Grand Palpa Stone were described by the lab as "not of recent origin."

However, as far as getting any exact dates for the stones the lab stated that "Patination is a relative dating method and is not absolute. These stones could have been engraved 500 years ago, 2000 years ago, or earlier, but definitely are not modern."

The researchers submitted the same three stones to another lab that used a different authentication methodology called metallurgical analysis, a procedure that examines the stone surfaces using dissection microscopes equipped with episcopic/incident light illumination (MIC)—a process that would not be influenced by any "artificial aging" patina applied to fake stones. Since the extract from the lab report in this article is a bit long and technical, I will just add their conclusion:

> This basaltic stone [stone of unknown provenance] showed small areas of copper mineralization loosely adhering to the regions of carved incision. The stone incisions also showed abrasion from incision. Although the stone indicated general protection from weathering, copper residues were severely weathered . . . The "weathering" on this stone [souvenir stone] peripheral to the incised figures was brushed on as a paint/coating.[2]

Although no dates were ascribed to the samples in this test, it was certain that the unknown provenance stone from Cabrera Museum showed indications that it was not a modern forgery, because the evidence of the "severe weathering" of copper residues on the stone.

Although I applaud the authors of the paper for using scientific methods for attempting to authenticate the stones, it seems like there needs to be more peer-reviewed testing to show that the rocks are indeed ancient. Some of these rocks were found in archaeology sites that are believed to be no older than 1700 years, which is still a ridiculously recent period of time to display men with dinosaurs. However, is it conceivable that a rock with a sauropod head carved on it (see fig. 12.5 p. 184) and excavated from a Nazca tomb that was dated between 400 and 700 CE was significantly older than the tomb site itself. It is plausible the Nazca people may have found these stones and kept them as revered and sacred items.

One further note about these stones. Though it was mentioned earlier in this section that our occultists claimed early humans were not threatened by predators because of their more ethereal bodies, many of

Fig. 12.4. A photo of the head of the dinosaur-like figure from Palpa Museum, with stone showing extensive patina buildup. Photo courtesy David Woetzel.

these stones obviously show men being eaten and attacked by bizarre-looking, dinosaur-like creatures (see fig. 12.6 below). If these stones are in fact authentic, I can only take this to mean that the people who rendered such a world on these rocks saw humans in their more physical stage of existence, which would be the last stages of Lemurian evolution, and the beginning of the Atlantean Epoch. Whether they saw these worlds through their physical eyes, or psychically, is another matter altogether.

Fig. 12.5. Ica Stone showing men with strange dinosaur-like creatures. Photo by David Woetzel. See also color plate 16.

## FONTAINEBLEAU: THE STONE FOREST

When I first saw images of the truly surreal and lifelike rock formations at the Stone Forest in Fontainebleau, France, I was equally blown away and flummoxed at the same time. I thought: How could these animal forms be natural, as the geologists who studied the rocks claim? Not only do the rocks show the uncanny forms of ancient animals—mostly reptilian—but they are anatomically correct too! The legs, eyes, and noses are where they should be, and the skin and scales look like something you would see on any reptile today. Also, there are very human-looking faces seen in the rock, with the most animated expressions one can imagine. They are screaming. They are mocking. They are laughing. They are bashful.

I do know that there is a very real psychological trait, which humans, and probably most animals, have, called pareidolia. This is a tendency to impose a meaningful interpretation on a nebulous stimulus, usually visual, so that one sees an object, pattern, or meaning where there is none. Okay, but I have personally never seen natural stone works mimic life and human emotions quite as realistically as these rocks do at Fontainebleau. Also, this rock forest has many such images, not just one or two.

Could it be that we are seeing something other than pareidolia here?

Fig. 12.6. Stone with fish-reptilian features, Fontainebleau, France. Photo by: Bruno Teste, Stone Jinns blog. See also color plate 17.

Figs. 12.7, 12.8. Fontainebleau, France.
Photo credit: Bruno Teste.

Fig. 12.9. Beasts in solid rock.
Photo credit: Bruno Teste.

Are we in fact seeing the work of a master Lemurian artist (or artists) molding forms out of rocks, using sound frequencies and imaginative imagery held by the hyper-concentrated mind of a master?

Let's assume that these are not natural formations, but the work of early humans possessed with enhanced psychic capabilities. Can you not see these stones rivaling some of the master works of the most exalted artists in history, in skill, beauty, and vision? There is a natural sophistication and quality to the work that makes these creations come alive—like God was forming bodies from the living rock. One might compare them to the works of Michelangelo or da Vinci in their life-like—albeit more abstract—beauty. If these were done with the power of the mind and sound, and not with tools, these would be significantly more incredible, as they would show a level of human development we can only dream of today.

If these were the works of artists, I wonder what they were thinking when they created these shapes. Were they just depicting the world around them or were they in fact co-creators with Source in the making of these forms? But, one might ask, how can rock be turned into something that looks like life itself?

Figs. 12.10, 12.11. Fontainebleau, France.
Photo credit: Bruno Teste.

Fig. 12.12. Fantastic face in stone.
Photo credit: Bruno Teste.

Maybe now would be a good time to mention the physicist and musician Ernst Chladni and his work with sound frequency and matter. Chladni was a brilliant visionary who believed all manifest life was an expression of frequency. His plate experiments showed that matter (sand on a metal plate) changed patterns when unique frequencies were applied, and every tone had a distinctive and repeatable pattern. This sound-visualization method is known today as cymatics, a term first coined by Hans Jenny, whose sound work followed in Chladni's footsteps.[3]

Today, modern sound experimenters are showing what can be done in three dimensions, using frequency on water and plasma. Not only are these organic-looking forms shaped just by using sound, but they show movement as well![4]

What science is demonstrating today is something the ancients knew very well, that sound (frequency) is the cause of manifestation. Remember, the first paragraph in the Bible is:

In the beginning was the Word, and the Word was with God, and the Word was God. The same was in the beginning with God. All

Fig.12.13. The Chladni Plates show distinctive patterns
for each frequency. Image by Chris Smith.

things were made by him; and without him was not any thing made
that was made.[5]

What is "Word" but frequency?

The masters of India called this primal sound by many names,
including Bani, Shabda, Nam, Om, or Hu, but in English we can call
this the "Audible Life Stream." Yogis say this Stream is nothing less
than the Supreme One, projecting into all planes of life in a constant
stream of musical vibrations, and through which flows the most incom-
prehensive power, life giving and creative.

Dr. Julian Johnson, who spent seven years learning and practicing
a Hindu theology called Sant Mat from the masters in India, said this
about the Audible Life Stream:

The Audible Life Stream is the cardinal, central fact in the Science
of the Masters. It is the keystone of the arch. It is the cornerstone
of the structure. It is the structure itself. And, it is the path of the

Masters. One might say that the Master and the Life Stream constitutes the Path of the Masters. The great spiritual current is not only the central fact in the Science of the Masters but it is the supreme fact and factor of the entire universe. It is the very essence and life of all things. . . .

By many ages of self-indulgences in these regions of gross matter, everyone has gotten himself out of tune with the infinite Stream of Life. This Stream, or wave, or current, is comparable to the electromagnetic wave of the radio. It fills all space around us and within us, but we do not know it, cannot hear it until we tune into harmony with it.[6]

We can also see that the ancient languages of Sanskrit and Hebrew are known to have root sounds represented for each letter in their alphabet, and each of these sounds holds a unique creative power and meaning. This is one of the reasons sacred texts say using this sound has a power to transform a person, especially with focused intention. For instance, when singing mantras using these root sounds, one is literally transforming one's body, mind, and soul. I have personally witnessed the power of sound and song to transform people in *kirtans* (places where people sing sacred chants and mantras), as well as in shamanic ceremonies. I have seen people spontaneously shake, cry, laugh, and sigh, sometimes uncontrollably, sometimes ecstatically.

One of the most memorable, transformative, and instructive moments for me was in an ayahuasca ceremony that I attended a few years back in the Sacred Valley of Peru. This ceremony demonstrated to me just how powerful sacred music, combined with sacred medicine, is to one's spiritual and physical being.

When our professionally trained musician and facilitator played Bach on her cello, one literally felt the music working through one's body at a psycho-spiritual level—I swayed and felt in a trance as the music worked on my soul in miraculous and mysterious ways. In addition to the ecstasy I felt as the sublime music worked on my soul,

I also understood that it worked on me on a deep cellular level. As the last note played from our gifted maestra's hands, my body felt as if it was so reconfigured that I could do nothing else but retch over and over again into my purge bowl. Such pleasure. Such pain. Such is the power of sound and sacred music on one's being.

What many don't understand is how the mind is all part of this. Your frequency and intention really do matter, and mind, according to the ancients, is in fact a type of matter. This is why your state of consciousness and your physical body can be so impacted during ceremony, as your daily defense mechanisms are turned off, or diminished. This happens when the ayahuasca molecules inhibit your MAO-beta-carbolines, which allow the DMT molecules to go past your blood-brain barrier, and you then begin to experience the effects of the medicine. When this happens, you begin to go inward, often to the vast depths of your soul. You begin to drop all the self-created barriers and veils that your ego has constructed to help you function and cope in the world. If you fight ayahuasca to hold on to this lower self, she usually will give you a good kick in the ass. This is when people get body ticks, shakes, and bouts of tears. As the shaman says: "let it all go and flow." Good advice for sure when it comes to your lower ego.

But, conversely, sometimes you need to turn on your mind to take control, especially when you become overwhelmed by intense visuals, which can be common during ceremonies.

In a particularly hard ceremony in California, where I participated in a two-night affair by drinking ayahuasca the first night, and huachuma (San Pedro cactus) the following, I realized that it was possible to shift my mind when things got a bit too intense for me. When I went to bed in my tent after the completion of the second night's ceremony, I got an overwhelming dose of psychedelic visuals—gyrating and spinning fractals and geometric patterns of intense colors, all shifting and moving intensely—which gave me an overwhelming sense of nausea. There also was a dark energy coming into my field of consciousness and I began to feel scared.

I have been a meditator for many years, and at this period I started to concentrate on something positive, and I called for guru Paramhansa Yogananda to help me in my time of distress. As soon as I redirected my focus and called for Yogananda my consciousness shifted, and a beautiful shimmering mandala of pulsing golden white light materialized before my very eyes. All the fear and nausea died away instantaneously. Did I just see Yogananda's energy pattern? I felt I did. From that moment on, the crazy visuals died down and the dark energies disappeared.

If the mind has such powers to control your reality, just imagine how we can control that chattering monkey of our brain swinging from branch to branch, always searching for better fruit and more stimulation. Mind control is something the masters of yoga have taught for ages. In Yogananda's famous book *Autobiography of a Yogi*, he described masters who had amazing, superhuman levels of mind control. He mentions yogis who could stand for days on end on one leg, slow down their vitals to the point of near death, and abstain from food for months. Others could manifest things on the physical plane. Such a level of mind control is unheard of in the West, where people are more used to chasing one new thrill after another. Little do they know the thrill of stillness, and the power of going within with focused concentration.

A little known secret in esoteric societies, as well as in certain spiritual communities, is the learning of techniques to not only change your personal nature through mind control but also to effect changes in the material world through focused concentration. I, for one, can't go much into this. I am not an adept nor a member of a secret society, but I am aware of these practices. I can say that this is a closely guarded secret for many good reasons on which I don't need to elaborate. However, I can say that beginners have to learn a great deal about mind control, and before doing so should be thoroughly vetted for personality defects—before getting the keys to these powers.

Even if you are not a member of such a society or religious group, you do affect and direct conditions in the world—albeit for most people, mainly in an unconscious way. We have all been conditioned to see the world from infancy to the grave through the lens of our parents, our education, and our peers, as well as by the messages the media beam to us. We need to ask: Are these perceptions accurate reflections of the truth? Are they designed to make you feel inadequate, or envious, in order to sell you a new product or idea? Are they designed to get you to believe that there is only one economic model that is viable? Are they designed to make you feel there are constant enemies out there and wars that have to be fought? Aren't these the messages that predominate reality today for many people?

As Shakespeare said, "All the world's a stage," and we all have our roles to play—or conversely, because of our will, not play. Since our consciousness is infinite, if we don't like the version of reality others are performing or asking us to perform, we could get off the stage and create something new. So why not make the world a more loving, more self-affirming, more beautiful one? Shift your consciousness and shift the world. We have that power if we believe we do.

# 13

# Tales of Lost Worlds

*Myths and legends, either about divinities or the formation of history of peoples and races, begin to look like pictures on a jigsaw puzzle, slightly different from one another but always built with the same pieces. Though not in the same order.*

CARLOS RUIZ ZAFON

Besides looking at the physical evidence at ancient sites and the writings from our Akashic seers, it would serve us well to analyze the legends and myths from Indigenous sources, and any manuscripts that have managed to survive, for more clues about our ancient past.

By exploring the oral traditions of different cultures we can use the process of comparative analysis to examine if a story has enough similarities in detail to a legend to discern if it is based on real events in the past. One of the best examples of an enduring and universal legend is the Great Flood story. It is claimed that there are more than five hundred catastrophic flood myths from around the world,[1] including the story of Noah's Ark, the Sumerian *Epic of Gilgamesh*, the Maya *Popol Vuh*, and the Hindu *Puranas*. Even the famous Greek philosopher Plato wrote in his dialogues *Timaeus* and *Critias* that the technologically advanced civilization of Atlantis sank, in a night and a day, into the ocean around 9,600 BCE. Can so many similar legends, frequently written down in foundational and sacred texts, just be a coincidence? It is highly doubtful. Most likely the survivors kept this event alive through oral histories and sacred texts to etch it in the minds of their descendants, to be told repeatedly over and over again, as a reminder to not commit the sins of their forefathers—or at least, to send a message that the Earth goes through significant geological changes periodically.

Although most people are aware of these global flood legends, they may not be cognizant that there were other equally catastrophic myths for humanity throughout Earth's hoary history. For instance, we hear in the Mesoamerican document the *Popol Vuh*, that humanity went through three destructions before the gods created a humankind they were happy with. The Hopi from North America also mention these three creations and destructions: the first world succumbed to fire, the second to ice, and the third to water, with a fourth catastrophe yet to come to humankind. The Greeks, Romans, and Persians also record a series of cyclical die-offs for humanity in the past.

Do these legends record the demise of ancient Lemuria (also known as Mu) and Atlantis and other catastrophes still unknown? Helena Blavatsky mentions that Mu and Atlantis experienced not just one such event, but multiple events over their respective epochs, with the most destructive of them putting a final end to their civilizations. Let's explore some of these stories.

## HESIOD'S AGES OF MAN

Hesiod's "ages of man" gives an account of the successive historical stages of human existence in Greek mythology. They progress from an original, long-gone time in which humans enjoyed a nearly divine existence to the current age of the writer, in which innumerable pains and evils beset humans. In the two accounts that survive from ancient Greece and Rome, this degradation of the human condition over time is indicated symbolically with metals of successively decreasing value.

Hesiod gives details of the multiple creations and destructions of the races that have come before humanity as we know it today. He begins with the Golden Race, followed in succession by a Silver Race, a Bronze Race, a Race of Heroes, and ends with the Iron Race, which is the one in which humanity currently resides.[2] It is said that Zeus sent a flood to destroy the Bronze Race, who were described as having the "strength of giants, and mighty hands on their mighty limbs."[3]

## OVID'S FOUR AGES

The Roman poet Ovid describes in his book *Metamorphoses* the four ages of human civilization, categorized into the Golden Age, the Silver Age, the Bronze Age, and the Iron Age. Ovid's Golden Age is described as a period where justice and peace reigned supreme, and humans lived off the bounty of the fertile Earth, which "freely, without the scars of ploughs, untouched by hoes, produced everything from herself." Ovid adds that "human beings only knew their own shores," feeling no desire to explore other worlds during this idyllic time.

In the Silver Age, the god Jupiter introduces the seasons, which would imply that the Earth somehow experienced a pole shift and most likely the one that gave us the 23.44 degree axial tilt that we see on the Earth today. Today we know that this tilt is the reason we have seasons. As a consequence of this environmental change humans began to adapt to the different conditions by learning the art of agriculture and architecture.

In the Bronze Age, Ovid only offers a brief description of human affairs saying that humans had "fiercer natures, readier to indulge in savage warfare, but [are] not yet vicious."

It was in the Iron Age that things started to go seriously south for humanity and Ovid writes that "every kind of wickedness erupted into this age of baser natures: truth, shame and honour vanished; in their place were fraud, deceit, and trickery, violence and pernicious desires."[4]

Despaired and angered by the degeneracy of humanity, Ovid describes an irate Jupiter who, with the help of his brother Neptune, sends down rain from the whole sky and drown humanity beneath the waves with a great flood."

Fig. 13.1. Neptune unleashes the Flood, The Metamorphoses.

## THE AVESTAN SCRIPTURES

The pre-Islamic Avestan scriptures from Persia have no fewer than sixteen different worlds created by Ahura Mazda, which were besieged by his nemesis Angra Mainyu—the evil one—who ended up corrupting humanity with several plagues to mar the native perfection of Ahura's creations. The first creation by Ahura Mazda conveys an idyllic time when the ancestors of the Persian peoples lived in the fabled Airyanan Vaejo, a paradise on Earth. But because the good god Ahura Mazda lost a battle with his nemesis Angra Mainyu, the land was quickly turned to an uninhabitable wasteland. From *Vendidad*, fargard one:

The first of the good lands and countries, which I, Ahura Mazda, create, was the Airyana Vaeja, but the Vanguhi Daitya. Thereupon came Angra Mainyu, who is all death, and he counter-created the serpent in the river and Winter, a work of the Daevas. There are ten winter months there, two summer months; and those are cold for the waters, cold for the earth, cold for the trees. Winter falls there, the worst of all plagues.[5]

And, fifteen times again, the good worlds created by Ahura Mazda are eventually destroyed by the evil and corrupting influences of Angra Mainyu.

When we get to fargard two, about the myths of Yima, we begin to see a flood tradition that closely parallels the story of Noah's Ark in the Torah. Here Ahura Mazda speaks to Yima, the chosen one, about preparing for the upcoming ice and deluge:

22. And Ahura Mazda spake unto Yima, saying: "O fair Yima, son of Vivanghat! Upon the material world the evil winters are about to fall, that shall bring the fierce, deadly frost; upon the material world the evil winters are about to fall, that shall make snow-flakes fall thick, even an aredvi deep on the highest tops of mountains.

23. And the beasts that live in the wilderness, and those that live on the tops of the mountains, and those that live in the bosom of the dale shall take shelter in underground abodes.

24. Before that winter, the country would bear plenty of grass for cattle, before the waters had flooded it. Now after the melting of the snow, O Yima, a place wherein the footprint of a sheep may be seen will be a wonder in the world.

25. Therefore make thee a Vara, long as a riding-ground on every side of the square, and thither bring the seeds of sheep and oxen, of men, of dogs, of birds, and of red blazing fires. Therefore make thee

a Vara, long as a riding-ground on every side of the square, to be an abode for man; a Vara, long as a riding-ground on every side of the square, for oxen and sheep."[6]

Here we note the word *vara*, a hypogeum or underground container, which will keep seed and life safe until the world has recovered and is ready to be reseeded again. The only discernible difference between the Bible's version and the Avestan texts is that the vara is underground instead of a floating ship.

■ ■ ■

In the next series of myths we jump across the pond and explore similar myths in the Americas.

## THE POPOL VUH

According to Scottish journalist, poet, author, folklorist, and occult scholar Lewis Spence, "There is no document of greater importance to the study of the pre-Columbian mythology of America than the Popol Vuh. It is the chief source of our knowledge of the mythology of the K'iché people of Central America, and it is further of considerable comparative value when studied in conjunction with the mythology of the Nahuatlacâ, or Mexican peoples."[7] This important document describes a series of creation and catastrophic events where the gods attempt, multiple times, to make a suitable humanity, but because of humanity's lack of reverence and errant ways, the gods turn on them and destroy their creations. Here is a passage from the first book of the Popol Vuh:

Over a universe wrapped in the gloom of a dense and primeval night passed the god Hurakan, the mighty wind. He called out "earth," and the solid land appeared. The chief gods took counsel; they were Hurakan, Gucumatz, the serpent covered with green feathers, and

Xpiyacoc and Xmucane, the mother and father gods. As the result of their deliberations, animals were created. But as yet man was not. To supply the deficiency the divine beings resolved to create mannikins carved out of wood. But these soon incurred the displeasure of the gods, who, irritated by their lack of reverence, resolved to destroy them. Then by the will of Hurakan, the Heart of Heaven, the waters were swollen, and a great flood came upon the mannikins of wood. They were drowned and a thick resin fell from heaven. The bird Xecotcovach tore out their eyes; the bird Camulatz cut off their heads; the bird Cotzbalam devoured their flesh; the bird Tecumbalam broke their bones and sinews and ground them into powder. Because they had not thought on Hurakan (God), therefore the face of the earth grew dark, and a pouring rain commenced, raining by day and by night.

Here is more:

After this catastrophe, ere yet the earth was quite recovered from the wrath of the gods, there existed a man "full of pride," whose name was Vukub-Cakix. The name signifies "Seven-times-the-colour-of-fire," or "Very brilliant," and was justified by the fact that its owner's eyes were of silver, his teeth of emerald, and other parts of his anatomy of precious metals. In his own opinion Vukub-Cakix's existence rendered unnecessary that of the sun and the moon, and this egoism so disgusted the gods that they resolved upon his overthrow. His two sons, Zipacna and Cabrakan (earth-heaper, and earthquake), were daily employed, the one in heaping up mountains, and the other in demolishing thorn, and these also incurred the wrath of the immortals. Shortly after the decision of the deities, the twin hero-gods Hun-Ahpu and Xbalanque came to earth with the intention of chastising the arrogance of Vukub-Cakix and his progeny.

But the *Popol Vuh* here is not speaking of the above humanity as the first real humans. That comes later, when the gods are seen once again in council discussing their latest creation:

> In the darkness they commune concerning the creation of man. The Creator and Former made four perfect men. These beings were wholly created from yellow and White maize. Their names were Balam-Quitzé (Tiger with the Sweet Smile), Balam-Agab (Tiger of the Night), Mahucutah (The Distinguished Name), and Iqi-Balam. (Tiger of the Moon). They had neither father nor mother, neither were they made by the ordinary agents in the work of creation. Their creation was a miracle of the Former.
>
> But Hurakan was not altogether satisfied with his handiwork. These men were too perfect. They knew overmuch. Therefore the gods took counsel as to how to proceed with man. They must not become as gods. Let us now contract their sight so that they may only be able to see a portion of the earth and be content, said the gods. Then Hurakan breathed a cloud over their eyes, which became partially veiled.

It seems as though these first "perfect" godlike men, who had no mother or father, and were not created by the "ordinary agents of creation," could have offspring. In the next part of the story, it relates how their ancestors met their demise, along with other races that the gods created. (Other versions say that these "other races" were Kichés too, but that they broke away into different tribes and spread out into the four corners of world):

> These were the ancestors of the Kichés only. Then were created the ancestors of other peoples. They were ignorant of the methods of worship, and lifting their eyes to heaven prayed to the Creator, the Former, for peaceable lives and the return of the sun. But no sun came, and they grew uneasy. So they set out for Tulan-Zuiva, or the

Seven Caves, and there gods were given unto them, each man, as head of a group of the race, a god. Balam-Quitzé received the god Tohil. Balam-Agab received the god Avilix, and Mahucutah the god Hacavitz. Iqi-Balam received a god, but as he had no family his god is not taken into account in the native mythology.

The story continues that the Kiché began to feel a need for fire—as of yet the land had no sun—so the fire god, Tohil (the Maya equivalent of Prometheus), supplied them with it. But soon afterward a mighty rain extinguished all the fires in the land. However, the benevolent Tohil always renewed their supply.

The land where these ancestors of the Kiché landed was not very hospitable and people continued to suffer through cold and famine. Also, the first four men (sometimes described as tribes) lost their ability to comprehend each other, as their speech was so confounded, that they decided to leave the cursed land to search for a new abode.

Eventually, after much struggle and hardship, they landed at Mount Hacavitz, named after one of their gods, and were instructed that they would see the sun again. "And the sun appeared. Animals and men were transported with delight. . . . But the sun was not as it is today. He was not strong, but as reflected in a mirror."

Over time the descendants of the first Kiché built a great city, but as the first Kiché got old, they began to have ominous visions, and began to offer human sacrifices to the gods. They raided the villages of the neighboring tribes, and these tribes retaliated, but "by the miraculous aid of a horde of wasps and hornets the Kichés utterly routed their enemies." The end of this humanity is recorded as such:

Now it came nigh the death-time of the first men, and they called their descendants together to hearken unto their last counsels. In the anguish of their hearts they sang the Kamucu, the song "We see," that they had sung when it first became light. Then they took leave of their wives and sons, one by one. And suddenly they were not. But in their place was a huge bundle, which was never unfolded. And it was called the "Majesty Enveloped." And so died the first men of the Kichés.[8]

## THE AZTECS

The Aztecs also had their recurring creation and destruction myth known as the legend of the Five Suns, which relates how their worlds, called "suns" had been created and destroyed four times before our present cycle—the fifth sun, which started at the time of Spanish colonization. The legend said that different gods governed the Earth in previous ages through a dominant element and sacrificed themselves to create a new world.

The First sun cycle the world was inhabited by giants "who ate only acorns" and were eventually devoured by jaguars thus ending this world; In the second sun cycle (wind) the world was governed by the featured serpent Quetzacoatl, and ended with terrible hurricanes and earthquakes after being dethroned by the god Tezcatlipoca; the third world (rain) whose ruling deity was the rain god Tlaloc, came to an end when Quetzacoatl unleashed rain of fire and ash; and the fourth world was governed by the goddess Chalchiuthlicue, who was the sister and wife of Tlaloc the aforementioned rain god. At this time, it was said that a great flood destroyed the world and turned humans into fish. Today, we are in the fifth sun era, ruled by the sun god Tonatiuh, under the daysign in the Aztec Calendar called Ollin (movement). This world is said to end by great earthquakes as well as by people being eaten by "sky monsters."

## SOUTH AMERICA

In South America there is a similar account of multiple race-destroying cataclysms by a vengeful god, Kon Tiki (Viracocha), who destroyed an unruly race of giants before creating human beings.

He made the sun, moon, and the stars. He made mankind by breathing into stones, but his first creation were brainless giants that displeased him. So, he destroyed them with a flood and made humans, beings who were better than the giants, from smaller stones. After creating them, they were scattered all over the world.[8]

Also, later it was recorded in a myth about a flood called Unu Pachakuti that human beings met a similar fate:

A large, rich city once existed on the Altiplano. One day, a group of ragged Indians came and warned the proud inhabitants that the city would be destroyed by earthquake, flood, and fire. Most inhabitants just scoffed and eventually had the ragged people flogged and thrown out. Some of the city's priests, though, heeded the warning and went to live as hermits in a temple on a hill. Some time later, a red cloud appeared on the horizon. Soon it had grown and covered the area, and its red glow eerily lit the night. Suddenly, with a flash and a rumble, an earthquake destroyed many of the city's buildings, and a red rain poured down. Other earthquakes and more rain followed, and a flood soon covered the ruined city; this water is Lake Titicaca today. None of the city's inhabitants survived save the priests. The descendants of the prophets became the Callawayas, wise men of the valleys.[9]

## THE HOPI

It is worth spending a bit of time on Hopi cosmogony, as the Hopi have an amazing oral history that is claimed to go back to the beginning of time for humanity. The Hopi are an Amerindian people of the Shoshóne group of the Uto-Aztecan linguistic family, and currently live on Indian reservations in northeastern Arizona, in the current territory of the United States.

Like the Aztecs and Mayans, the history of the Hopi speaks of four ages of the world, and the time in which we live currently is the fourth age. They also have prophecies as to the future worlds that will come. According to Hopi cosmogony, multiple cycles of devastation befell humanity:

> According to the Hopi tradition, the history of Humanity is divided into Worlds, separated from each other by natural catastrophes. The first world succumbed to fire, the second to ice, and the third to water. Our current world is the fourth and, according to their prophecies, it is coming to an end, and will give way to a new world in the not too distant future. In total, Humanity will have to go through seven periods.[10]

Interestingly, this belief matches what Helena Blavatsky has said about the seven races of man—that they will go through seven evolutionary cycles in which each subsequent race will come forth after some catastrophe from the preceding time. Blavatsky writes:

> Every root-race is separated by a catastrophe, a cataclysm—the basis and historical foundation of the fables woven later on into the religious fabric of every people, whether civilized or savage, under the names of "deluges," "showers of fire," "great floods" and the like.

According to the Hopi, we are currently going through the fourth cycle on Earth and it is nearing an end, and their prophecies say this about signs we will see before our end times:

> If we dig precious things from the land, we will invite disaster. . . . Near the day of Purification, there will be cobwebs spun back and forth in the sky. . . . A container of ashes might one day be thrown from the sky, which could burn the land and boil the oceans.[12]

Although these accounts sound very bleak, the Hopi mention that if one stays on the correct path by remembering and honoring the Creator, as well as respecting and living in balance with the Earth and its people, the Creator will show mercy to his children.

## THE KACHINA AND THE ANT PEOPLE

Hopi cosmogony also has a much-repeated symbolism seen in destruction legends all over the world: that helper gods, the *kachinas*—and, in the case of the Hopi, Ant People—intervene to save and guide the chosen people. Not only do these helpers take people to new lands, but they also teach them the skills to start civilization anew after some major catastrophe. Here author, independent researcher, and archaeoastronomer Gary A. David describes how the Ant People saved humanity not just once, but twice:

> The so-called "First World" (or world-age) was apparently destroyed by fire—possibly some sort of volcanism, asteroid strike, or coronal mass ejection from the sun. The Second World was destroyed by ice—Ice Age glaciers or a pole shift. During these two global cataclysms, the virtuous members of the Hopi tribe were guided by an odd-shaped cloud during the day and a moving star at night that led them to the sky god named Sotuknang, who finally took them to the Ant People—in Hopi, Anu Sinom. The Ant People then escorted the Hopi into subterranean caves where they found refuge and sustenance.[13]

In this legend, the Ant People were said to be industrious and generous, and when the humans found themselves low on food they gave up some of their own supplies so that humans wouldn't starve. The legend relates that this is why the Ant People have such thin waists. The story goes on to say that they also advised humans on the merits of storing food for future times.

Fig. 13.2. Rock drawings of the Ant People who
help save the Hopi in times of catastrophe.

Besides the generous Ant People, the Hopi have the kachinas—
elite corporeal beings (some say they were spirit beings) from the planet
Toonaotekha—as spiritual allies. Their oral history says that several
millennia ago the ancestors of the Hopi once lived on a continent in
the Pacific they called Kasskara. When a war broke out with another
continent, and Kasskara began to sink into the ocean, the Hopi emi-
grated to another place with the help of the kachinas—even though the
kachinas' planet was a long way from their own solar system. However,
that did not prevent them from making regular visits to Earth on their
flying shields (*patuwvotas*).

I found something quite interesting about these space visitors—
especially in the context of writing this book and exploring how the
ancients made the megalithic works around the world—and that is
that the kachinas were known to have mastered the abilities to cut and
transport stone and build underground facilities:

The Hopi claim that their ancestors were visited by beings from the stars that moved on flying shields or thundering birds, who mastered the art of cutting and transporting huge blocks of stone, as well as building tunnels and underground facilities. These were the kachinas (or katchinas), which means, wise, illustrious and respected.

The Kachinas saved the Hopi people from one of these cataclysms and thus they learned to observe the stars, cut roots, about animals, plants, community life. They multiplied as a people, and from them new clans arose that spread throughout America. The Kachinas helped the chosen ones to move to new lands.[14]

Could these kachinas be the "Seven Sages" that we hear about in so many other myths around the world—from Egypt, to Mesopotamia, to Easter Island—who give humans the practical skills and knowledge to help them rebuild the world after some sort of cataclysm? Some legends say that these sages were survivors of Atlantis—but perhaps, originally, they came from much farther away.

## PROUD CITIES AT THE BOTTOM OF THE SEA

According to the book *Following the Path of Peace*, these words were spoken by Sotuknang (the nephew of the Hopis supreme god, Taiowa) at the beginning of the Fourth World:

See, I have washed away even the footprints of your Emergence; the stepping-stones which I left for you. Down on the bottom of the seas lie all the proud cities, the flying patuwvotas [shields], and the worldly treasures corrupted with evil, and those people who found no time to sing the praises to the Creator from the tops of their hills. But the day will come, if you preserve the memory and the meaning of your Emergence, when these stepping-stones will emerge again to prove the truth you speak.[15]

One thing I notice in the above passage is that "stepping-stones" is repeated twice. What are these stepping-stones, and why was it so important that the Hopi remember them? According to author Boyé Lafayette De Mente, these stepping-stones were islands that the Hopi used to reach the Fourth World:

> Sotunkang then instructed the Hopis to look westward to the islands that they used as stepping stones to reach the Fourth World, and while they were watching he caused the islands, which were actually the tops of mountains and were all that remained of the Third World, to sink beneath the waves, bringing the final end to the Third World.[16]

I couldn't help but notice that the description by Sotunkang of the Third World civilization at the bottom of the sea closely resembles Plato's description of Atlantis's demise. In his *Critias* dialogue, Critias speaks of the remnants of Atlantis after its destruction: "There are remaining only the bones of the wasted body, as they maybe called, as in the case of small islands, all the richer and softer parts of the soil have fallen away, and the mere skeleton of the land being left."

Though Plato doesn't mention flying shields in his dialogues, in India it was recorded in their most sacred texts that the ancients did fly around in flying shields called *vimanas*. The vimanas first appeared in the Vedas, and had several meanings ranging from "temple" or "palace" to mythological "flying machine." (It seems more than likely that all the words apply to describe the vimana, as it was means of transportation for the Gods, and pictures depicting them do look rather palatial.) Hindu scripture also say that they were used in warfare as well as space and underwater travel.[17]

Going back to the Hopi legend of the destruction of the Third World, it seems strange that the legend relates how Sotuknang left these flying shields on the bottom of the ocean, while in another legend, the kachinas were said to visit Earth from their home planet on them. It is even said that at the end of the Fourth World some Hopi will leave the Earth on these shields.[18] Was it possible that these flying shields may have been a technology transfer from the kachinas to the Atlanteans some time in the past? It is possible that the kachinas deemed it safe to do so when the Atlanteans were "moral" and "spiritual" in the beginning? If they did share technology with the Atlanteans, is it possible that Sotunkang destroyed these flying shields to send a message to the kachinas that it is best not to give advanced technology to humans because they will eventually abuse these gifts?

## THE FOURTH WORLD ACCORDING TO GRANDPA DAN

In one incredible narrative about the coming end times, Frank Waters records the legend of the "Blue Star Kachina" in the *Book of the Hopi*. The story came from Grandfather Dan Evenham, a respected Hopi elder and medicine man. It is worth quoting in its entirety as we can see some chilling similarities to our own times:

Many will seem to have lost their souls in these final days. So intense will be the nature of the changes that those who are weak in spiritual awareness will go mad, for we are nothing without spirit. They will disappear, as they are just hollow containers that anything can use. Life will be so bad in the cities that many will choose to leave this plane. Some in whole groups.

Only those who return to the values of the old ways will be able to find peace of mind. Because on Earth we have to find relief from the madness that will be around us. It will be a hard time for women with children, because they will be avoided, and many of the children in these times will be unnatural. Some will be beings from the Stars, others from past worlds, and still others artificially created by man and will be soulless. Many of the people at this time will be empty in Spirit, they will have *Sampacu*. No life force in his eyes.

As we get closer to the time of the arrival of the Purifier there will be those who walk like ghosts through the cities, through the ravines that they will have built in their man-made mountains. Those who walk through these places will be very heavy in their walk, it will seem almost painful to take each step, as they will be disconnected from their spirit and the Earth.

After the arrival of the twins (the red and blue Kachinas), they will begin to disappear before your eyes like so much smoke. Others will have great deformities, both in mind and in their bodies. There will be those who will walk in a body that is not of this reality, since many of the portals (gateways) that once protected us will be opened, there will be a lot of confusion. Confusion between the sexes, and children and their elders.

Life will become very perverted, and there will be little social order, in those times many will ask the mountains themselves to fall on them and put an end to their misery. Still others will appear as if they are not touched by what is happening. Those who remember the original teachings and have reconnected their hearts and spirits. Those who remember who their mother and father are. The Pahana (the Lost White Brother) who has gone to live in the mountains and forests.[19]

If we take these myths as anything but fiction, it is hard to escape the message that the Earth has been visited by many catastrophes in its past. It is also undeniable that there is a moral lesson associated with these events. It is repeated over and over again, and says that if we do not mend our ways by living in harmony with the Earth and with each other, and by remembering and honoring our creator, then God will cleanse the Earth until we learn these lessons.

# 14

# Examples of Hanan and Uran Pacha Sites around the World

It wasn't until I discovered Vlad9vt's channel on YouTube that I discovered that Hanan Pacha and Uran Pacha work was literally everywhere—not just in Peru, but all over the planet. Though Alfredo Gamarra had mentioned that these monoliths and megaliths were found all around the world, it is much more compelling to see so many examples in video, and still images, and Vlad's YouTube channel is the mother lode for this type of research.

Vlad equally sees these sites as mysterious and worth championing, and he has spent many years documenting, commenting on, and producing videos featuring these strange rock formations. I am deeply grateful for his wonderful body of work compiling videos that show just how prevalent these sites are.

The nice thing about having this abundant evidence is that it puts to rest the idea that this style or building was solely done by the Inca, Greeks, or the Egyptians, as we can find these types of wakas at sites all over the world. This also gives credence to the idea that we are talking about a worldwide culture that is at play here, and this backs up

Gamarra's and Steiner's theories of an early civilization that covered the globe in the ancient past.

I compiled some of the best photos of these sites below. All images, unless specified, are fair use creative commons, with the photographer's name if available. I've decided not to put a section here for Peru, as many of the photos in this book are from that country. For abbreviation and space, I have neglected many countries that have Hanan Pacha and Uran Pacha work, as it would fill up an entire book.

# THE MIDDLE EAST

## *Turkey*

Fig. 14.1. Lion's Gate, Hattusha. Photo by Bernard Gagnon.
See also color plate 18.

Fig. 14.2. Alacahoyek polygonal wall. Photo by A_O_C.

Fig. 14.3. Hattusha Great Temple with green stone.
Photo by Murat Özsoy.

Fig. 14.4. Yazilikaya.
Photo by Murat Özsoy.

# *Iran*

Iran is most famous for its Persepolis temple, which was considered the ceremonial capital of the Achaemenid Empire (c.550–330 BCE). It was believed that Cyrus the Great chose this site and that Darius I built the terraces and the palaces. Beneath the very ornate columns, statues, and palaces are huge megaliths, many of them polygonal. Did Cyrus choose this site because he recognized the importance of the civilization that built the foundation stones?

Fig. 14.5. Bistoun, Iran. Photo by Armin Amirian.

Fig. 14.6. Ruins of the Tachara, also known as the "Palace of Darius," in Persepolis, Iran.

Fig. 14.7 & Fig. 14.8. Naqsh-e Rostam.
Photos by Carole Raddato.

Fig. 14.9. The monument of Qadamgah in present-day Iran.
Photo by ynamosquito.

Fig. 14.10. Tachara, in the Temple of Darius, Iran.
Photo by Seyed M. Afzouni.

## *Lebanon*

The Baalbek Quarry is probably one of the most famous places in the world for megalith lovers. Here one can find massive stone blocks, the largest measuring 64 feet by 19.6 feet and is 18 feet tall and estimated to weigh 1,650 tons.

Fig. 14.11. Baalbek Quarry.
Photo by Lodo27.

Fig. 14.12. Baalbek Quarry.
Photo by Lodo27.

Fig. 14.13. West Wall of Temple Complexes in Baalbek Quarry.
Photo by Lodo27.

## *Palestine/Israel*

Fig. 14.14. The "Foundation Stone" under the Dome of the Rock.
Photo by Carole Raddato.

Fig. 14.15. Wailing Wall.
Photo by Dainis Matiso.

## *Jordan*

Little Petra in Jordan sees evidence of overbuilding. A more modern temple facade is constructed over an ancient cave system with classic Hanan Pacha style niches and shapes cut or formed into the stone.

Fig. 14.16. Little Petra, Jordan.
Photo by Anastasia Pozdnyakova.

## _Egypt_

Fig. 14.17. Zawyet el-Aryan.
Photo by MONNIER Franck.

Fig. 14.18. Pyramid of Menkaure.
Note knobs on stones are very similar to those in Peru.

Fig. 14.19. Temple of Seti. Photo by Merlin UK.

Fig. 14.20. Osirion.
Photo by Olaf Tausch.

# ASIA

## *China*

Probably the biggest Hanan Pacha site in the world, the so-called Yangshan "Quarry" has evidence of geopolymer use and knobs that are commonly seen in Peru.

Fig. 14.21. Yangshan Quarry, China.

Fig. 14.22. Yangshan Quarry, China.

Fig. 14.23. Yangshan Quarry, China.
Photo by Vmenkov.

Fig. 14.24. Yangshan Quarry, China. See the knobs angled up,
which doesn't make sense if you were lifting stones.
Photo by Vmenkov.

## *Japan*

I found Japan to be one of the most fascinating places when it comes to Hanan Pacha work, holding some of the most beautiful examples I have seen outside of Peru.

Fig. 14.25. Sakafune-ishi, Honshu.
Photo by Aska, The Megalithic Portal website.

Fig. 14.26. Oni no Manaita.
Photo by Kansai explorer.

Fig. 14.27 & Fig. 14.28. Front and back part of the
"Masuda no Iwafune" megalith or "rock ship" at Asuka.

Fig. 14.29 & Fig. 14.30. The "Ishi no Hoden" Shrine, Takasago, Japan.
The rock above weighs around five hundred to six hundred tons.
Photo by z tanuki. See also plates 19 and 20.

Fig. 14.31. The "Ishi no Hoden" shrine rock, Kufun.
Photo by Saigen Jiro.

Fig. 14.32. Kameishi Monolith.
Photo by +−.

Fig. 14.33. Amazing monolith with the inglorious
name of "The Devil's Toilet."

Fig. 14.34. Asuka, Japan.
See also color plate 21.

Fig. 14.35 & Fig. 14.36. Banbaura Stone Quarry.
Photos from Jcastle.info.

Fig. 14.37. Tako-ishi, Osaka-jo castle.
Photo by lasta29.

Fig. 14.38. Large Stone at Kyobashi-Guchi entrance to Osaka Castle.
Photo by Ethan Doyle White.

## *Southeast Asia*

Fig. 14.39. Aik Renung Megalithic site, Indonesia.

Fig. 14.40. Wat Phu Champasak, Laos.
Photo by Mattun0211.

## *India*

The archaeological sites called the Udaygira and Khandagiri caves in India show classic signs of overbuilding with evidence of later civilizations building on top of a foundation of first world construction. What is surprising is that there is actual proof that this was the case with the discovery of the Hathi Gumpha Inscription found in the cave of the same name. The inscription reads that the first century BCE king (Kharavela) was "the worshipper of all religious orders, the repairer of all shrines of gods."

Fig. 14.41. Barabar caves.
Photo by Abhisal2408.

Fig. 14.42. Udayagiri and Khadagiri caves.
Photo by Phadke09.

Fig. 14.43. Khadagiri cave.
Photo by Gbmukherji.

Fig. 14.44. Barabar caves in Sudama.
Photo from Hidden Inca Tours.

Fig. 14.45. Ellora caves. Photo by Saurabh Koravi.
See also color plate 22.

# EUROPE

## *Italy*

Fig. 14.46. Fucen's polygonal masonry.
Photo by Roger Ulrich.

Fig. 14.47. Pietra Pertosa.
Photo by Alessio020302.

Fig. 14.48 & Fig. 14.49. Bomarzo pyramid, Italy.
Photos courtesy of Giulia Marchetti.

## *Greece*

A Hanan Pacha style monolith seems to be the foundation of the Acropolis, Greece's most famous temple. Opposite the temple is a site known as the Pnyx, which shows the unmistakable shapes and forms that make up the first world construction. Here, an old painting by Edward Dodwell shows its relationship to Acropolis. Also featured around the Hanan Pacha work is a retaining wall of polygonal megaliths, which is a common site seen in Peru.

Fig. 14.50. *Pnyx* by Edward Dodwell (1767–1832).

Fig. 14.51. The Retaining Wall of the Pnyx.
Photo by George E. Koronaios.

Fig. 14.52. Pynx, Athens. Photo by Mirjanamimi.

Fig. 14.53. The Solar Clock of Meton on the Pnyx.
Photo by George E. Koronaios.

## *Sardinia*

Fig. 14.54 & Fig. 14.55. Irru's sacred pit in Nulvi.
Photos by Sergio Melis.

## Portugal

The similarities of the monolithic work seen at the Sanctuary of Panóias in Portugal with those found in Peru and Bolivia are striking, including the stairways winding up to the top where one can find perfectly shaped holes, niches, and basins.

Fig. 14.56. Panóias Sanctuary.
Photo by João Carvalho.

Fig. 14.57. Santuário de Panóias.
Photo by João Carvalho.

Fig. 14.58. Panóias Sanctuary.
Photo by Armond.

# *Bulgaria*

Fig. 14.59. Perperikon Water Reservoir. Photo by Guido van Beurden.
See also color plate 23.

Fig. 14.60. Perperikon. Photo by Ben Lee.
See also color plate 24.

Fig. 14.61. Sanctuary of Tatul known as the "Sanctuary of Orpheus."
Photo by Bin im Garten.

Fig. 14.62. Sanctuary of Tatul, also known as the "Tomb of Orpheus."
Photo by Vassia Atanassova. Public domain.

# THE AMERICAS

## *Bolivia*

Fig. 14.63. El Fuerte. Samaipata, Bolivia. Photo by Mhwater.
See also color plate 25.

Fig. 14.64. Samaipata, Bolivia. Photo by Dan Lundberg.
See also color plate 26.

## *Mexico*

I was quite surprised to see that Mexico had a considerable amount of Hanan Pacha work, some as fine as at Tiwanaku, Bolivia.

Fig. 14.65 & Fig. 14.66. San Miguel, Ixtapan, Mexico.
Photos from ARXprojectMX on Facebook.

Fig. 14.67. Tetzcotzinco, San Dieguito Xochimanca, Mexico.
See also color plate 27.

# Conclusion

For years I had this belief that there wasn't much to write about that hasn't already been said in the millions (or billions?) of books sitting in book shelves and on hard drives all around in the world. I thought, hasn't every topic been covered in infinite detail and now available in books, podcasts, documentaries, and scientific journals, just a library visit, or a Google click, away?

Fortunately, I was relieved to find out how wrong I was. Even with such an immense amount of knowledge and information at our fingertips there are still new discoveries happening every day that are not only changing the conversation but are groundbreaking. It turns out that all that new information is also fueling new insights that are prodding us to question the official narratives about our world, our history, and our nature.

Today we have many authors and content creators who are thinking out of the box of convention, and giving us fresh and new interpretations regarding the history of this planet and our unique story on it. Do they have a right to do so since many of them have no credentials in the topics they discuss? Some may say no. But we should reflect on the times in history where the authorities got things very wrong, like in the early seventeenth century when the church persecuted those who believed in heliocentrism, or how the eugenics movement was based on falsified science to benefit the dominant race, and, more recently, how authorities prescribed disastrous "solutions" for the covid pandemic. If only we listened to the heretics!

Though some may say that the church's persecution of "heretics", or the bad policies and bad science during the eugenics movement and the recent pandemic, have nothing to do with interpretations of history, I would say that we shouldn't be so naive. After all, if we don't point out in the geological record, as well as in ancient catastrophe legends, the evidence of recurring events that wiped out ancient civilizations, or the misuse of technology and magic that saw the ruin of ancient Atlantis, are we really learning history's lessons?

Today those topics are still mainly not discussed by mainstream historians and archaeologists, as the flood stories and fables of Atlantis are just that—fables and not to be taken too seriously. Others, like Graham Hancock, are saying we need to pay attention. These revelations are just too important for humanity and life on this planet to be ignored.

Of course, history—including fables—are our teachers, and there are still countless lessons to be learned from them, including the monuments that ancient civilizations have left behind. These are not just forgotten artifacts of a bygone day that hold no value to modern humanity but are tools for our inner development—to heal us and reconnect us again to the earth and our spiritual natures.

Sacred site researcher Freddy Silva says that most of these sites are constructed with stones that have significant piezoelectric and magnetic properties and sit in locations with strong telluric currents that, when combined, give off strong energy fields that can transform us. These sites are still very much alive and waiting for us to rediscover them.

Should I get the chance to write a second book, I would love to have the expertise of professional dowsers and scientists who can measure these sites for earth energy fields, as well as their function, which are topics that I touch upon in this book. Right now, I can only speculate about their properties and purposes because I lack the scientific background, and tools, to take measurements of them. The one thing I can say for sure that I truly know is how I feel around them . . . and it is a special kind of energy, and it is quite powerful.

Because I feel strongly that this type of research should be done on these sites, I have reached out to a well-known dowser from the UK and had a conversation with her about coming to do some field research. Hopefully, she can find some time in her busy schedule to come and do this investigation. I also contacted members of the Biogeometry community asking if anyone would be interested in doing studies on sites here in Peru.

Biogeometry is a relatively new science created by Egyptian architect Ibrahim Karim. This discipline uses ancient Egyptian esoteric knowledge of the qualities of shape, angle, proportion, and sound to create subtle energetic changes in the environment to balance and harmonize our bodies' electric fields.

Since Hanan Pacha (First World) constructions are so filled with so many obscure shapes, forms, proportions, and angles, I thought if I could find an expert in this field, one willing to come to Peru, then maybe we could get some answers as to the functions of these monuments. I have heard back from two people who are students of biogeometry, one being an advanced practitioner. Both are interested in coming to Peru to do fieldwork to investigate these sites using this unique science.

It is my profound hope that this book might generate more interest and serious study of these monuments. Though there has been significant work by researchers analyzing geomagnetic fields at sacred sites in other countries, especially in England, Europe, Russia, and Egypt, I haven't heard about such work being done here in Peru. Maybe this book may spark some interest by earth energy experts to venture down to the Southern Hemisphere to examine these beautiful and amazing sites as I feel we are just scratching the surface of their true power and purpose.

# Notes

## INTRODUCTION

1. De la Vega, *Historia*, 1:23.
2. De Leon, *Cronica del Peru*.
3. Steiner, *Atlantis*, 11.
4. Hammer, "What Is Beneath."
5. Zohar Vayechi 1:231; Midrash Tanchuma Acharei Ch. 3 (see Etz Yosef commentary); Maimonides, Beis HaBechirah 4:1.

## I. THE COSMOGONY OF THE THREE WORLDS

1. Hancock, *Magicians of the Gods*, 369.
2. Cartwright, "Sacsayhuaman."
3. Zora-Carvajal, "Revelan que restos preíncas."
4. Myers, "Inka archaeology."
5. De la Vega, *The Incas*, 290.
6. Myers, "Inka archaeology."
7. De Jong, "Archaeological proofs."
8. De Jong, "Home."
9. De Jong, "Mind Over Matter."

## 2. THE EXPANDING EARTH TIMELINE

1. Herbert, "Charles Darwin."
2. Tesla, "Expanding Sun."
3. Yarkovsky, "Hypothèse cinétique."

4. Newton, *The Third Book of Opticks*, 324.

5. Noel, "Continental Drift."

# 3. THREE WORLDS, THREE ORBITS?

1. Daley, "Earth's orbital shifts."

2. Callier, "Geologic evidence."

3. "Mass extinction."

4. Mason, "Devonian Death From Outer Space."

5. Hoffman, "The Permian Extinction."

6. Olsen, "Causes and Consequences."

7. Walkden, "Late Triassic Impact," 23.

8. Cowen, "The K-T Extinction."

9. Berkowitz, "NASA's DART mission."

10. Justin Me, "Aztec Calendar."

11. Hirst, "Mesoamerican Calendar."

12. Milbrath, "Maya Astronomical Observations."

13. Bellamy, *The Calendar of Tiahuanaco*.

14. MacLean, "The Gate of the Sun Calendar."

15. Justin Me, "Aztec Calendar."

16. De Jong, *The Discoveries of Alfredo Gamarra*.

17. "The CHAKANA or INCA CROSS."

18. Lundquist, "Borobudur."

19. Davidovits, "Ancient geopolymer in South American monuments."

# 4. FEELING HIGH? WAKAS AND ALTERED STATES

1. Silva, "They're Alive!"

2. Silva, "Naupa Iglesia."

3. Silva, "They're Alive!"

4. Méreaux, *Carnac*.

5. Giannoulopoulou, "Effects of Geophysical Anomalies."

6. Avia, "Abd'el Hakim Awyan."

7. Jeffers, "Investigating water supply at Saqsaywaman."

8. Burke, *Seed of Knowledge*, 8.

9. Burke, *Seed of Knowledge*, 24.

10. Erickson, "Raised Field Agriculture in the Lake Titicaca Basin," 9.

11. Pajares G., et al, "Relational knowledge systems," 213–232.

## 5. CHAMBERS FOR INITIATION

1. Silva, "Naupa Iglesia."

2. Garcés, *Astronomia inka*.

3. Silva, "Naupa Iglesia."

## 6. SACRED SITES AND SOUND HEALING

1. Hale, *Sacred Space*.

2. Reid, "Sound Healing."

3. Avia, "Abd'el Hakim Awyan."

4. Reid, "Sound Healing."

5. Reid, "Sound Healing."

6. MegalithomaniaUK, "Sillustani."

7. *Divine Blueprint*, 178.

8. Narby, *The Cosmic Serpent*, chapter 10.

9. Gadbois, "DNA."

10. Emoto, *The Hidden Messages in Water*.

## 7. DID ACOUSTIC LEVITATION MOVE THE MEGALITHS?

1. Palombo, "Pyramid Power."

2. Cathie, "Acoustic Levitation Of Stones."

3. Hedvallen, "How Tibetans used acoustic levitation of stones."

4. Pruitt, "Nikola Tesla's Missing Files."

5. Orlowski, "Free Energy Inventors."

6. Hedvallen, "How Tibetans used acoustic levitation of stones."

7. *Wired*, "Scientist Explains."

8. University of Bristol, "Most powerful acoustic tractor beam."

9. Sparkes, "Acoustic levitation."

10. Esposito, "Gravitational Mass Carried by Sound Waves."

11. Ancient Code Team, "Did Ancient Civilizations 'Levitate' Boulders."

12. Putney, "Piezoelectric Basins for Acoustic Levitation."

13. Al-Mas'udi, *The Meadows of Gold and Mines of Gems.*

14. Putney, "Piezoelectric Basins for Acoustic Levitation."

## 8. PROOF OF GEOPOLYMERS USED

1. "Georadar Research of Sacsayhuaman Archaeological Complex."

2. ISIDA Project, "Plasticine Stones of Sacsayhuaman."

3. World of Antiquity, "SACSAYHUAMAN."

4. De la Vega, *The Incas*, 288.

5. "Ollantaytambo: an architectural jewel."

6. Posnansky, *Tihuanacu.*

7. Davidovits, "Ancient geopolymer in South American monuments."

8. Juanjo Perez, *Los ablandadores de piedras,* September 2, 2006, accessed October 8, 2022.

9. Davidovits, "Ancient geopolymer in South American monuments."

10. Andrews, "Hydraulics of the Ancients."

11. Brien Foerster, "Astonishing Inca Stone Scale Model Of A City?"

12. Berninger, "The Surprising Truth."

## 9. EVIDENCE OF VITRIFICATION

1. De Jong, "Evidence of Vitrified Stonework."

2. Watkins, "Rock Chips."

3. Clark, "Atomic and Physical Properties."

## 10. THE VIEWERS: STEINER, BLAVATSKY, AND SUBRAMUNIYA

1. "Rudolf Steiner (1861–1925)."

2. Todeschi, "Mystic Edgar Cayce."

3. "What Are Akashic Records?"

4. Steiner, *Cosmic Memory.*

5. Hancock, *America Before.*

6. Blavatsky, *Secret Doctrine*, Vol 2, 46.

7. Blavatsky, "The Lost Atlantis."

8. Silva, *Divine Blueprint*, 202.

9. Brown, "Water Has Memory."

10. Blavatsky, *Secret Doctrine*, Vol 2, .224.

11. "Satguru Sivaya Subramuniyaswami."

12. Klostermaier, Klaus, *A Survey of Hinduism*, 231.

13. Subramuniyaswami, *Lemurian Scrolls*, 60.

## 11. TIME: RELATIVELY SPEAKING

1. Blavatsky, *The Secret Doctrine* (1999), 72.

2. Subramuniyaswami, *Lemurian Scrolls*, 60

3. Cayce, *Edgar Cayce on Atlantis*, 49

4. Rudolf Steiner, *Cosmic Memory,* 25.

5. Rudolf Steiner, *Cosmic Memory,* 33.

6. Subramuniyaswami, *Lemurian Scrolls*, 60, 266.

7. Blavatsky, *The Secret Doctrine* (1999), 159.

8. Blavatsky, *The Secret Doctrine* (1999), 329.

9. Blavatsky, *The Secret Doctrine* (1999), 317.

10. "Eocene Epoch."

11. "Miocene Epoch."

12. Blavatsky, *The Secret Doctrine* (1999), 157.

13. McInerney, "The Paleocene-Eocene Thermal Maximum."

14. "Study of Ancient Climate Suggests Warming Could Accelerate as $CO_2$ Levels Rise."

15. "The First Primates."

16. "Eocene Epoch."

17. "Eocene Epoch."

18. "Leaf It to the Experts."

19. Judge, *Echoes from the Orient*, 42–43.

20. Blavatsky, *The Secret Doctrine* (1999), 337.

21. "Lemuria," Theosophy Wiki.

22. Blavatsky, *The Secret Doctrine* (1999), 9.

23. "Tertiary Period."

24. Blavatsky, *The Secret Doctrine* (1999), 10.

25. Blavatsky, *The Secret Doctrine* (1999), 8.

26. "Cambrian Period," Wikipedia.

27. Subramuniyaswami, *Lemurian Scrolls*, 247.

28. Subramuniyaswami, *Lemurian Scrolls*, 246.

29. Subramuniyaswami, *Lemurian Scrolls*, 246.

30. Subramuniyaswami, *Lemurian Scrolls*, 246.

31. Subramuniyaswami, *Lemurian Scrolls*, 246.

32. Le Page, "Controversial Fossils."

33. Marzoli, "Extensive 200-million-year-old continental flood basalts."

34. Blavatsky, *The Secret Doctrine* (1999), 353.

35. Blavatsky, *The Secret Doctrine* (1999), 221.

36. Blavatsky, *The Secret Doctrine* (1999), 227.

## 12. STONE ODDITIES

1. "Sauropod Tracks."

2. Woetzel, "Ica Stones."

3. Jenny, *Cymatics*.

4. Zen Sound, "Water Sound Images of a Gong"

5. *Holy Bible: King James Version*, Genesis 1:1–2.

6. Johnson, *The Path of the Masters*, 175, 344.

## 13. TALES OF LOST WORLDS

1. Hancock, *Fingerprints of the Gods*, 190.

2. Buxton, The *Complete World of Greek Mythology*, 54.

3. Kerényi, *The Gods of the Greeks*, 226.

4. Ovid. *The Metamorphoses*, 89–150.

5. Peterson, *Avesta: Vendidad*, Fargard 1.

6. Peterson, *Avesta: Vendidad*, Fargard 2.

7. Spence, *The Popol Vuh*, 214.

8. Spence, *The Popol Vuh*, 218, 220, 232, 235.

7. Vail, *Re-Creating Primordial Time*, 31.

8. "Viracocha."

9. Gifford, *Warriors, Gods & Spirits*, 55–56.

10. "El Universo de los Hopi y su arte."

11. "The Seven Root Races."

12. "Native American Prophecies."

13. David, "The Ant People of the Hopi."

14. "El Universo de los Hopi y su arte."

15. Wilson, *Hopi: Following the Path of Peace*, 1994.

16. Mente, *America's Famous Hopi Indians!*, 33.

17. Chopra, "Vimana: The Ancient Indian Aerospace Craft."

18. Black, "Hopi legends and the 'flying shields.'"

19. Waters, *The Book of the Hopi.*

# Bibliography

Al-Mas'udi. *The Meadows of Gold and Mines of Gems.*

Ancient Code Team. "Did Ancient Civilizations 'Levitate' Boulders into Position and Build Massive Monuments?" *The Ancient Code.* Accessed October 8, 2022.

Andrews Sr., Dr. Arlan. "Hydraulics of the Ancients." *Atlantis Rising Magazine*, Jul. 2006.

Avia. "Abd'el Hakim Awyan, Mystical Wisdom-Keeper." *Egyptexperience*, June 9, 2011.

Bellamy H. S., and P. Allan. *The Calendar of Tiahuanaco: A Disquisition on the Time Measuring System of the Oldest Civilization in the World.* Faber and Faber, 1956.

Berkowitz, Bonnie. "NASA's DART mission will test a planetary defense strategy by smacking an asteroid." *The Washington Post*, November 21, 2021.

Berninger, Sheila, and Dorilona Rose. "The Surprising Truth Behind the Construction of the Great Pyramids." *National Science Foundation*, May 18, 2007.

Black, John. "Hopi legends and the 'flying shields.'" *Ancient Origins*, November 18, 2013.

Blavatsky, Helena P. "The Lost Atlantis." *THEOSOPHY* 42, no. 2 (Dec. 1952): 76–81.

———. *The Secret Doctrine: The Synthesis of Science, Religion, and Philosophy.* Theosophical University Press, 1999.

———. *The Secret Doctrine, Vol. 1 of 2: The Synthesis of Science, Religion, and Philosophy.* London: Forgotten Books, 2008.

Brien Foerster. "Astonishing Inca Stone Scale Model Of A City? Dr. Arlan Andrews Explains." *YouTube,* April 16, 2012. Brown, William. "Scientists Show that Water Has Memory." Reasonance Science blog. October 4, 2018.

Burke, John A. and Kal Halberg, *Seed of Knowledge, Stone of Plenty: Understanding the Lost Technology of the Ancient Megalith-Builders.* Council Oak Books, 2005

Buxton, R. G. A. *The Complete World of Greek Mythology.* Thames & Hudson, 2004

Callier, Viviane. "Geologic evidence confirms existence of 405,000-year Milankovitch cycle." *EARTH Magazine*, May 11, 2018.

Cartwright, Mark. "Sacsayhuaman," *World History Encyclopedia*, July 20, 2016.

Cathie, Bruce. "Acoustic Levitation Of Stones." *Becoming Borealis*, May 2, 2020.

Cayce, Edgar. *Edgar Cayce on Atlantis.* Warner Books 1968.

"The CHAKANA or INCA CROSS: a wonderful mystic and cultural symbol of the Incas." *Tour in Peru*, September 14, 2017.

Chopra, Anil. "Vimana: The Ancient Indian Aerospace Craft—Time for Indigenisation." *Air Power Asia*, August 27, 2020.

Clark, Jim. "Atomic and Physical Properties of the Period 3 Elements." *chemguide*. Accessed October 8, 2022.

Cowen, Richard. "The K-T Extinction." from *History of Life*. Boston: Blackwell Science, 2000.

Daley, James. "Earth's orbital shifts may have triggered ancient global warming." *Scientific American*, September 3, 2019.

David, Gary, "The Ant People of the Hopi" from *Ancient Origins*, October 13, 2013.

Davidovits, J., L. Huaman, and R. Davidovits. "Ancient geopolymer in South American monuments. SEM and petrographic evidence." *Materials Letters* 235, no. 15 (2019): 120-124. DOI:

De Jong, Jan Peter. "The Archaeological proofs on a DVD, explaining the ancient mysteries of the Inca vestiges." *Ancient Mysterious Explained.* Accessed October 10, 2022.

———. *The Discoveries of Alfredo Gamarra.* Accessed October 10, 2022.

———. "Home." *Ancient Mysteries Explained*. Accessed October 10, 2022.

———. "Mind Over Matter." Accessed October 10, 2022. *Jan Peter de Jong* website.

De Jong, Jan Peter, and Christopher Jordan. "Evidence of Vitrified Stonework in the Inca Vestiges of Peru." *Shan Newspaper*, December 14, 2011.

De la Vega, Garcilaso. *Historia General del Peru*. Madrid, Spain: Madrid Oficina Real, 1722.

———. *The Incas: The Royal Commentaries of the Inca*. Discus, 1971.

De Leon, Pedro Cieza. *Parte Primera de la Cronica del Peru*. Sevilla, Spain: Por Martin de Montesdoca, 1553.

Emoto, M. *The Hidden Messages in Water*. New York: Simon and Schuster, 2011.

"Enuma Elish, The Sumerian Epic of Creation." Accessed October 8, 2022.

"Eocene Epoch." *Encyclopedia Britannica*. Accessed October 8, 2022.

Erickson, Clark L. "Raised Field Agriculture in the Lake Titicaca Basin: Putting Ancient Agriculture Back to Work," *Expedition*, Vol. 30, 1988.

Esposito, A., R. Krichevsky, and A. Nicolis. "Gravitational Mass Carried by Sound Waves." *Physical Review Letters* 122, no. 8 (Mar. 2019). DOI: 10.1103/physrevlett.122.084501.

"The First Primates." Accessed via *Wayback Machine*, October 8, 2022.

Gadbois, Linda. "DNA - The Phantom Effect, Quantum Hologram and the Etheric Body." *MOJ Proteomics & Bioinformatics* 7, no. 1 (Jan. 2018). DOI: 10.15406/mojpb.2018.07.00206.

Garcés, E. S. . *Astronomia inka: arqueoastronomia y etnoastronomía*. 2021. Andrés Del Castillo Museum.

"The Georadar Research of Sacsayhuaman Archaeological Complex." *GPR Investigation*. Accessed October 8, 2022.

Giannoulopoulou L., A. Evangelou, S. Karkabounas, and S. Papamarinopoulos, "The Effects of Geophysical Anomalies on Biology." *Journal of Scientific Exploration* 32, no. 3 (Sep. 2018): 495–513. DOI: 10.31275/2018.1295.

Gifford, Douglas. *Warriors, Gods & Spirits from Central & South American Mythology*. Glasgow: William Collins, 1983.

Gupta, S. V. "Ch. 1.2.4 Time Measurements." In Hull, Robert, Richard M. Osgood Jr., Jurgen Parisi, Hans Warlimont (eds.). *Units of Measurement:*

*Past, Present and Future. International System of Units.* Springer Series in Materials Science: 122. 2009.

Hale, Susan Elizabeth. *Sacred Space, Sacred Sound: The Acoustic Mysteries of Holy Places.* Wheaton, IL: Quest Books. 2007.

Hammer, Joshua. "What Is Beneath the Temple Mount?" *Smithsonian Magazine*, March 31, 2011.

Hancock, Graham. *America Before: The Key to Earth's Lost Civilization.* New York: St. Martin's Press, 2019.

———. *Fingerprints of the Gods: The Evidence of Earth's Lost Civilization.* Crown, 2012.

———. *Magicians of the Gods: Fingerprints of the Gods.* Coronet, 2016.

Hedvallen, "'How Tibetans used acoustic levitation of stones' - Lost Technology, Henry Kjellson." Forum on *Graham Hancock.* Accessed October 8, 2022.

Herbert, Sandra. "Charles Darwin as a prospective geological author." *The British Journal for the History of Science* 24, no. 2 (June 1991): 159–192. DOI: 10.1017/s0007087400027060.

Hirst, K. K. "Mesoamerican Calendar: Tracking Time in the Ancient Mesoamerican World." *ThoughtCo*, March 13, 2010. *Holy Bible: King James Version.*

Hoffman, H. J. "The Permian Extinction—When Life Nearly Came to an End." *National Geographic*, December 2, 2009.

ISIDA Project. "Plasticine Stones of Sacsayhuaman." YouTube, May 5, 2016.

Jeffers, Olivia. "Investigating water supply at Saqsaywaman: A literature review of Incan water and drainage at Saqsaywaman." May 2013.

Jenny, Hans. *Cymatics: A Study of Wave Phenomena and Vibration.* Compilation of the original two volumes. Eliot, ME: MACROmedia Publishing. 2001.

Johnson, Julian P. *The Path of the Masters: The Science of Surat Shabd Yoga.* Radha Soami Satsang Beas, 1939.

Judge, William Q. *Echoes from the Orient.* Theosophical University Press, 1973.

Justin Me. "Aztec Calendar." YouTube, April 13, 2018.

Kerényi, Karoly. *The Gods of the Greeks.* London: Thames & Hudson, 1974.

Klostermaier, Klaus. *A Survey of Hinduism*. 3rd edition. SUNY Press, 2007.

"Leaf It to the Experts: Studying Plants to Understand an Ancient Global Warming Event," *WTTW*. Accessed October 8, 2022.

Lundquist, J. M. "Borobudur: The Top Plan and the Upper Terraces." *East and West* 45, no. 1/4 (December 1995): 283–304.

MacLean, K. "The Gate of the Sun Calendar from Ancient Tiwanacu." *World Mysteries Blog*. Accessed October 10, 2022.

Marzoli, A., et al. "Extensive 200-million-year-old continental flood basalts of the Central Atlantic Magmatic Province." *Science* 284 (April 23, 1999): 618–620.

Mason, Betsy. "Devonian Death From Outer Space." *American Association for the Advancement of Science*, June 13, 2003.

"Mass extinction." *Dictionary.com*.

McCarthy, D., "Biogeographical and geological evidence for a smaller, completely-enclosed Pacific Basin in the Late Cretaceous." *Journal of Biogeography*, 32 (2005): 2161–2177.

McInerney, F. A. and S. L. Wing. "The Paleocene-Eocene Thermal Maximum: A Perturbation of Carbon Cycle, Climate, and Biosphere with Implications for the Future." *Annual Review of Earth and Planetary Sciences*, 39, no. 1. (May 2011): 489–516, DOI: 10.1146/annurev-earth-040610-133431.

MegalithomaniaUK. "Sillustani," YouTube, March 26, 2022.

Mente, B. L. D. *America's Famous Hopi Indians!: Their Spiritual Way of Life & Incredible Prophecies!* Cultural-Insight Books, 2010.

Méreaux, Pierre. *Carnac, A Door to the Unknown*. Robert Laffont, 1981.

Milbrath, S. "Maya Astronomical Observations and the Agricultural Cycle in the Postclassic Madrid Codex." *Ancient Mesoamerica* 28, no. 2: 489–505.

Myers, Albert. "Inka archaeology and the Late horizon. Some polemic remarks." *ResearchGate*. Accessed October 10, 2022.

Narby, Jeremy. *The Cosmic Serpent*. New York: Penguin, 1999.

"Native American Prophecies." *IAWWAI*. Accessed October 8, 2022.

Newton, Isaac., *The Third Book of Opticks, Or, A Treatise of the Reflections, Refractions, Inflexions and Colours of Light*. 2nd ed., 1718.

Noel, David. "Continental Drift And Earth Expansion." AOI website. Accessed October 10, 2022.

"Ollantaytambo: an architectural jewel on the way to Machu Picchu." *Commission for the Promotion of Peruvian Exports and Tourism.* Accessed October 8, 2022.

Olsen, P. E., J. H. Whiteside, and P. Huber. "Causes and Consequences of the Triassic-Jurassic Mass Extinction as Seen from the Hartford Basin." Report, Columbia Climate School Lamont-Doherty Earth Observatory, 2003.

Orlowski, Gerald. "Too Many Free Energy Inventors Suddenly Dropping Dead & Disappearing!" *Peak Oil* message board. Accessed October 8, 2022.

Ovid. *The Metamorphoses.* Trans. A. S. Kline. CreateSpace, 2014.

Pajares G., Erick & Larrabure, Jaime. "Relational knowledge systems and their impact on management of mountain ecosystems: Approaches to understanding the motivations and expectations of traditional farmers in the maintenance of biodiversity zones in the Andes." *Management of Environmental Quality, An International Journal,* 22, 2011. 10.1108/14777831111113392.

Palombo, Anthony, citing David Wilcox. "Pyramid Power Page 3: Acoustic Levitation." *Healing Tones.* Accessed October 8, 2022.

Peterson, Joseph H. (digital preparation). *Avesta: Vendidad.* Accessed October 8, 2022.

Posnansky, Arthur. *Tihuanacu, the Cradle of American Man.* J. J. Augustin, New York. 1945

Pritchard, James B., ed. *The Ancient Near East, Volume 1: An Anthology of Texts and Pictures.* Princeton: Princeton University Press, 1958.

Pruitt, Sarah. "The Mystery of Nikola Tesla's Missing Files," *History,* May 3, 2018.

Putney, Alex. "Piezoelectric Basins for Acoustic Levitation Identified at Megalithic Sites." *Human-Resonance.org.* Accessed October 8, 2022.

Reid, Annaliese and John Stuart. "Sound Healing - Ancient Sounds." *Token Rock.* Accessed October 8, 2022.

"Rudolf Steiner (1861–1925)." *Biblio,* Accessed October 8, 2022.

"Satguru Sivaya Subramuniyaswami." *Kauai's Hindu Monastery.* Accessed October 8, 2022.

"Sauropod Tracks." *Cleveland Museum of Natural History.* Accessed June 26, 2022.

"The Seven Root Races." *Bodhaya*. Accessed October 8, 2022.

Silva, Freddy. *The Divine Blueprint: Temples, Power Places, and the Global Plan to Shape the Human Soul*. Invisible Temple, ebook. 2016.

———. "Naupa Iglesia. A Portal in the Andes." *Invisible Temple*. Accessed October 10, 2022.

———. "They're Alive! Megalithic Sites Are More than Just Stone." *Ancient Origins*, September 11, 2021.

Sparkes, Matthew. "Acoustic levitation used to build complex structures in mid-air." *New Scientist*, June 29, 2022.

Spence, Lewis. *The Popol Vuh: The Mythic and Heroic Sagas of the Kichés of Central America*. London: David Nutt, at the Sign of the Phoenix, 1908.

Steiner, Rudolf. *Atlantis: The Fate of a Lost Land and Its Secret Knowledge*. Rudolf Steiner Press, 2013.

Steiner, Rudolf. *Cosmic Memory*. Hudson, NY: Steiner Books, 2006.

Subramuniyaswami, S. S. *Lemurian Scrolls: Angelic Prophecies Revealing Human Origins*. Himalayan Academy Publications, 2006.

"Tertiary Period." *Encyclopedia Britannica*. Accessed October 8, 2022.

Tesla, Nikola. "Expanding Sun Will Explode Some Day, Tesla Predicts." *New York Herald Tribune*, August 18, 1935. Accessed on *Wikisource*.

Todeschi, Kevin J. "Mystic Edgar Cayce Explains the Akashic Records." *Omega Institute*, August 3, 2018.

"El Universo de los Hopi y su arte." *Consejo Interamericano Sobre Espiritualidad Indigena*, November 12, 2013.

University of Bristol. "The world's most powerful acoustic tractor beam could pave the way for levitating humans." *ScienceDaily*. Accessed October 8, 2022.

Vail, Gabrielle and Christine Hernández. *Re-Creating Primordial Time: Foundation Rituals and Mythology in the Postclassic Maya Codices*. University Press of Colorado, 2013.

"Viracocha," *Bloomsbury Dictionary of Myth*. London: Bloomsbury Publishing Ltd., 1996.

Walkden, G., J. Parker, and S. Kelley, "A Late Triassic Impact Ejecta Layer in Southwestern Britain." *New Scientist Magazine*, February 8, 1992.

Waters, Frank. *The Book of the Hopi*. Penguin Books, 1977.

Watkins, I. W. "Rock Chips." *Rocks & Minerals* 65, no. 6 (Nov. 1990): 541–544.

"What Are Akashic Records?" *Akashic Studies Australia.* Accessed October 8, 2022.

Wikipedia, "Cambrian Period."

Wilson, Terry P. *Hopi: Following the Path of Peace.* San Francisco: Chronicle Press, 1994.

*Wired.* "Scientist Explains How to Levitate Objects With Sound," YouTube, January 28, 2022.

Woetzel, David and Dennis Swift. "Can the Ica Stones be independently authenticated?" *Creation Ministries International.* Accessed October 8, 2022.

World of Antiquity, "SACSAYHUAMAN - How They Did It." YouTube, September 12, 2021.

Yarkovsky, Ivan Osipovich. "Hypothèse cinétique de la Gravitation universelle et la connexion avec la formation des éléments chimiques." Moscow, 1888.

ZEN SOUND. "Water Sound Images of a Gong by Alexander Lauterwasser." YouTube, May 27, 2014.

Zora-Carvajal, Fernando. "Revelan que restos preíncas conforman el 40% del Parque Arqueológico de Machu Picchu." *Agencia Peruana de Noticias Andina.* Accessed October 10, 2022.

# Index

Numbers in *italics* preceded by *pl.* indicate color insert plate numbers.